D1650229

AUTHOR | **CLASS**

TITLE

a30118 0353180906

Cuckoo

A Play

Emlyn Williams

Samuel French – London
New York – Sydney – Toronto – Hollywood

CUCKOO

Cuckoo was first presented, by Michael Redington, at the Yvonne Arnaud Theatre, Guildford, on 31st May 1986, with the following cast:

Madam, Cuckoo's aunt	Lila Kaye
Benjy	Karl Howman
Cuckoo	Rosemary Leach
Jerome	Anthony Smee
Powell, Cuckoo's uncle	John Stratton
Lydia, Cuckoo's sister	Tessa Peake-Jones
Mrs Dix	Doreen Andrew

The play directed by the Author

Setting by Eileen Diss
Costumes by Liz Gilbert
Personal Assistant to the Director Brian Tipping

The action takes place in a bungalow on a small island in the Thames, near Hampton Court

ACT I
SCENE 1   A morning in May
SCENE 2   Five weeks later; an afternoon in July

ACT II
SCENE 1   Some hours later, near midnight
SCENE 2   The next morning

Time—1935

To
Rosemary Leach and
Michael Redington

AUTHOR'S NOTE

In this, the published play, I have included specially detailed stage directions—as to acting, setting and movement—based on the original production, with the idea that they may be useful to directors up against the problem of "the time element".

Emlyn Williams

ACT I*

A bungalow on a small island in the Thames, near Hampton Court. The time is 1935, a fine morning in May

The living-room R *occupies roughly three-quarters of the set. The remaining quarter is composed of the veranda, with a glimpse of greenery and a couple of garden bushes. In the* R *wall, downstage, the kitchen door; higher upstage, in the same wall, a door leading to Mam's bedroom (called "the bedroom door"). In the back wall of the room,* R, *an archway leads to a corridor going left and right. Opposite the archway, is the door to Madam's room; Powell's bedroom is off the corridor to* R, *and out of sight. In the back wall, to* L, *the fireplace, a fan of paper in the grate. In the wall* L, *upstage, the main window of the room; next to it, downstage an open glass door gives access to the veranda, and thence to the bit of garden and the river*

The veranda looks rickety and the building is of the cheapest kind, with walls and slanting roof of distempered beaver-boarding, but the room avoids the sordid; the distemper wants renewing, but it is a pleasant mellow colour. The crowded room is higgledy-piggledy with furniture and ornaments of mixed styles; cheap bungalow bits jostle against old solid pieces; a couple of warm landscapes

Between the fireplace and the veranda, facing, a Welsh dresser with china; near it a plant and an old dinner-gong. Below it, against the veranda wall, a dining-table with four chairs. Near the dresser, a tray, on end. Next to Madam's door, a shabby hatstand; a few hats and coats. Against the R *wall, between kitchen and bedroom, a good-looking desk and desk-chair. On the desk, a telephone of the period, the receiver at the end of a cord, and a wireless set. Over the desk, bookshelves. In the middle of the room,* DS, *a stool (or pouffe) and armchair; between them, a small (low) table. Sitting upright on the stool, a large doll, very old and partially bald, white-faced and shabbily dressed in light colours. Behind, half-facing the fireplace, a sofa. Oil lamps, with cheap unobtrusive shades. On the veranda, a couple of garden chairs and tables, very shabby*

Before the CURTAIN *rises, light music of the period. This continues as the action begins, fainter and proceeding from the waterway* L. *Both bedroom and kitchen doors are open. On the dining-table, the remains of breakfast*

---

*N.B. Paragraph 3 on page ii of this Acting Edition regarding photocopying and video-recording should be carefully read.

Madam is seated at a table on the veranda, pecking at a small typewriter. She is a somewhat faded beauty, between fifty and sixty, with too much make-up and too-striking hair, dressed in a once-garish kimono which she carries off with brio. A woman who has slid into bad days but will not admit it, she is gallant and infuriating, lovable and bristling with pretence. She has a habit of adopting a shaky but accomplished Italian accent as she comes out with stray foreign expressions. At other moments, there are faint Welsh intonations

Benjy stands at the telephone, hanging on. He is a healthy burly young cockney who has been many things in his time, the calling most easily guessed at being that of the sea. He has natural good manners, but loves life and is unlikely to be nonplussed. He wears the trousers of an old suit, and an old sweater; he is in shirt-sleeves and carries a duster in his belt

A pause. Madam types, the music plays. She puts her hands to her ears

Madam That River Thames! Every other punt carries a portable gramophone, *orribile* . . . (*She types as the music dies away*)

Benjy (*into the telephone*) Fishmonger? . . . Mornin', miss, I'm speakin' on be'alf of the Roberts family, could you send six fillets o' plaice. . . . No, miss, this is the new maid. Checked in a couple of hours back, from the Labour Exchange an' learnin' fast, name o' Benjy. . . . (*Calling, to Madam*) Excuse me, is this Cozy Cot?

Madam I'm afraid so, with two Ks. (*She types*)

Benjy (*into the telephone*) It is. . . . No, miss the lady of the 'ouse went into 'orspital yesterday, the report is satisfactory——

Madam My sister will be home Monday week.

Benjy (*into the telephone*) Back Monday week, thank yew. (*He is about to replace the receiver*)

Madam How do you spell "absinthe"? You know, the drink, absinthe, it's for my Life Story. (*Designating the typewriter*)

Benjy (*after hesitating, into the telephone*) Do me a favour, miss, 'ow d'you spell "absinthe"? . . . (*Calling, to Madam*) A,b,s,e,n,t . . .

As Madam types the letters . . .

(*Into the telephone*) Thank you, miss, six plaice, righty-ho . . . (*He puts back the receiver and dusts the telephone*)

Madam (*reading*) "From the moment I had sung at the Paris Opéra-Comique, my favourite drink and ever-present friend-in-need was absent", it doesn't look right. (*Taking up a batch of script*) Ah well, press on, turn me on a bath, *caro*, will you?

Benjy (*going up to clear breakfast*) Can't at the moment, Madarm.

Madam Why not?

Benjy There's a clothes-'orse in it.

Madam Oh. Take the horse right out of the bath and ride it straight back to the stables.

Benjy looks back at her, and decides he has not heard aright

From the bedroom, suddenly, Cuckoo's voice, singing absentmindedly, cheerfully, on the shrill side

Cuckoo (*off*) "Funny ole London, Jolly ole town . . ."
Benjy (*peering through the open door, amused*) 'Ello 'ello 'ello . . .

A pause, then Cuckoo wanders in. She is a robust, wholesome, pretty woman, between thirty-five and forty, dressed in a nondescript, colourless shift, too long and too loose, under a bedraggled cardigan; sandals, worn and heavy. Since she is shiningly clean, there is nothing sordid in her appearance; it is merely old-fashioned, dowdy. She wears a faded old sunbonnet and a small handbag is attached to her wrist. Her gait is curious—slow and uncertain, yet not ungraceful; the uncertainty—between sudden movements of impetuous gesture—betrays the fact that she is mentally retarded. But there is nothing pitiable about her; her face, innocent of make-up, framed by straight bobbed hair, like a schoolgirl, is the face of a child. Her mind, too, is the mind of a child: a bright child. She is a happy creature, with—habitually—an air of wide-eyed thoughtful serenity. The sun-bonnet is curiously becoming, in the style of the silent cinema

Cuckoo (*advancing, singing the same jingle, nonchalantly*) "Funny ole London, Jolly ole town . . . In for a penny, in for a poun' . . ." (*The cockney is artfully exaggerated*)
Madam Mind the chair, dear . . .

She is a second too late to stop Cuckoo banging slightly into the desk-chair. Cuckoo sits on the edge of the chair, and looks at the telephone. Her expression is suddenly dejected, puzzled. Benjy watches her, fascinated. Slowly she reaches forward and puts out a hand

Benjy No . . .
Madam (*who has been typing intermittently*) Darling, leave the telly-phony aloney . . . Misses her mother, poor child . . . (*She continues typing*)
Benjy (*looking at the doll, then addressing Cuckoo*) Where's Daisy?

No answer; he steps nearer, then hands on knees:

Where's Daisy, ducks?
Cuckoo Having a nice s-sitdown. (*She speaks with little difficulty, though slowly and with an intermittent stammer. Her accent is indeterminate, with a basis of Welsh. From the desk, she takes up a simple piece of knitting, and knits*)
Benjy (*looking at the doll*) Oh yes. White as a sheet, she must be poorly.
Cuckoo Waiting for the telly-phony.
Benjy O' course she is. They tole me all about you in the Labour Exchange. 'Ow many thruppeny bits you got?

Cuckoo shakes her handbag: the rattle of a money-box inside it

'Ow many hats you got?
Cuckoo S-seven.
Benjy Clever girl. (*He goes back to the dining-table*)
Cuckoo Madam s-sing. (*A pause*) Sing?
Madam Not now dear, I'm writing my Life Story.
Cuckoo Sing?

Madam (*singing, mechanically, while studying her script*) *Caro nome che'l mio cor, festilente palpitar* ... (*Rising showing off to Cuckoo, according to custom*) Tellyphony please to me, We'll have hot-cross buns for tea!

Cuckoo claps her hands

(*Peering out over the garden*) Those people in the punt, look at them staring, they think I'm mad ... (*Booming defiantly, arm extended as a Valkyrie*) Yo-ho-ho-*ho*! Yo-ho-ho-*ho*! (*She sits again and types*)

Benjy Where are you now Madarm, got to the Scala Milan yet?

Madam Monte Car-rlo, I can smell the cigars. This is me on the Dolly Sisters, big stars they were, the talk of the Casino. (*Reading, from her script*) "They glanced up from the baccarat table to make a note of my daring dress, as with a flick of a wrist they lost a cool million."

Benjy I bet *you* was a star, too!

Madam I sang some very nice roles.

Benjy When was Monte Carlo, Madarm?

Madam Let me see—when was the war?

Benjy Finished in nineteen-eighteen, so I'm told. Eighteen from nineteen-thirty-five—seventeen years back.

Madam Oh dear ... The Victory Ball, Dame Clara Butt singing "Land of Hope and ..." *Sapristi*, seems like yesterday ...

Cuckoo turns on the wireless

Cuckoo What's a w-war?

Madam It's when people kill each other, dear (*She types a word*)

Cuckoo Why?

Madam Because it was the war to end all wars. (*She types*)

Nondescript music creeps in, on the wireless

No dear, on Thursdays it doesn't come on till the afternoon ...

Benjy What's that?

Madam An absurd programme called "Funny Ole London", she was singing the theme song just now ...

Benjy That's right, I know it ...

Madam Lots of silly voices, *molto comico*. Mind you, she'll listen to anything on the wireless for hours, picks up phrases, you'd be surprised. (*Typing*) Switch it off Benjy, there's a dear ...

The music fades out. As Benjy crosses to the wireless:

Man's voice (*on the wireless*) "The weather. It will be mostly sunny all day, with temperatures ranging between ..."

Benjy switches off the wireless, and returns to the dining-table

Cuckoo (*mechanically, a passable imitation of the silken tones*) Later there will be a deep depression over Iceland and most of the Fairy Islands. (*Shrill cockney*) Won't 'arf be cold, oo-er ...

Madam That's "Funny Ole London" ... (*Typing a last word, then rising, decisively*) There ... (*Taking up her bag*)

Cuckoo, who has put down her knitting, looks at the telephone with a sigh

Benjy Won't ring by jus' lookin' at it, y'know. You jus' got to be patient.

Madam (*coming into the room*) *Assez de travail!* (*Sinking into the armchair*) I'd give anything for a champagne cocktail ... (*Closing her eyes*)

Cuckoo rises, comes down to the stool, takes Daisy up as if she were a baby, and goes into the bedroom, leaving the door again open

Madam is powdering her face. A knock on the (open) kitchen door

Avanti ...

Jerome enters. He is a good-looking man in his early thirties, dressed unobtrusively in (summer) city clothes; he wears a hat, which he takes off; he carries a parcel. His self-possession is charming and unconscious

Benjy studies him closely

Jerome Sorry to come in through the kitchen ...

Madam (*Italian*) It is the only way, unless you tr-ravel by the river.

Jerome This *is* Kozy Kot?

Madam *Si si*, isn't it nauseating? We've got used to it, over the years—we can do even better, next door we have the Robinsons.

Jerome What's theirs called?

Madam Nest O'Robinsons. Are you insurance? My sister's away ...

Jerome I'm a friend of her daughter's.

Madam Lydia? She's not here.

Jerome Not here? (*Put out*) But when I rang the office in Ludgate Circus they told me she's at home ...

Madam Well, she is and she is not—Lydia is down the river visiting her mother in Kingston Hospital, home later.

Jerome Good ...

Madam Would you like me to give her a message.

Jerome No thank you—(*crisply*)—I'd like to give her a message.

Madam Oh?

As Benjy crosses to the kitchen, with his tray

Jerome I want to marry her.

Madam stares at him: Benjy too

Madam Sit down.

Jerome Thank you. (*He puts down his hat and parcel, and sits on the stool*)

Madam You must be the one she calls her pick-up!

Jerome (*not amused*) Does she now? ... We met in the Tube.

Benjy One more for lunch, Madarm?

Madam Of course ...

Benjy And excuse me Madarm—if you could pop in an' show me where all the stuff goes?

Madam *Subito, caro ...*

Benjy Ta.

He goes into the kitchen

Madam How long have you been in love with her?
Jerome Since we met, in the Tube. Six weeks ago.
Madam You are *sentimentale*, I find that *simpatico*!
Jerome It's not *sentimentale*, it's what happened.
Madam Ah ... (*Rising, and walking up towards the archway*) I must announce to my brother ... (*Calling, excited*) Powell, a visitor! (*Back*) And Lydia has said yes!
Jerome No.
Madam No? (*Incredulous*) She has said *no*?
Jerome No. She hasn't said anything.

As Madam sits

I wrote her last week, twice, no answer. No contact—nothing—that's why I'm here. (*He is, for him, het up*)
Madam She has quite a shy side, *nostra* Lydia ...

Powell enters from his room: that is, from R of the archway; he is seated in his old wheelchair, which he propels with skill. He is a studious man in his late forties, shabby but fine-looking, with a cheerful easy eloquence. From the waist down, his body is hidden by a rug. All about him is neat and clean, but worn: clothes, rug, chair. The chair has a home-made tray attached to it, with books and notebooks

Powell A visitor, did you say?
Madam Powell dear, this is Mr——
Jerome Price, Jerome Price ...
Madam He wants to marry Lydia.
Powell Oh? (*Putting on spectacles, suspended round his neck by a cord*) I'm her mother's brother. (*Studying Jerome*) And very nice too.
Madam He's here to propose to her.
Powell And have a look at all of us, can't blame him. Kozy Kot, Mr Price, is the seat of the house of Roberts-Ellis, a stronghold of Welsh émigrés in Bungalowland. You may wonder where Madam comes in. Madam Gwendolen Ellis is an international operatic orchid from Methodist soil. Our sister has talked broken French in Rome, broken Italian in Paris, and in London she's broken both.
Madam (*giggling*) Powell ...
Powell What else? ... You may have gathered that we're ... not well off. They say wealth corrupts—if it does, the house of Roberts-Ellis looks pretty safe to me.
Madam (*to Jerome*) Have *you* any money?
Jerome I ... I work in an office too.
Madam Oh.
Jerome I have ... prospects.
Powell That sounds promising, we might settle for it ...
Madam (*remembering*) Ah ... (*Rising*) The kitchen ...
Powell Is there something about a wheelchair that makes it run people's lives?

Jerome (*as Madam crosses*) You've had an accident?

Madam stops at the kitchen door

Powell (*amiably*) I'm still looking for a way to answer that without embarrassing.

Jerome Oh ... (*Confused*) I'm sorry——

Madam My brother, Mr Price, was wounded in the Great War.

She goes into the kitchen, leaving the door open

Powell Do sit down ...

As Jerome sits again, on the stool

In case you visualize the Charge of the Light Brigade ... the truth is that one fine evening on a beach off the River Somme, I disregarded the signs and went for a walk. It was my last, my legs couldn't be found anywhere. Might have been worse, I was never an athlete and used to trudge down country lanes longing for a lift. You could say that I have—that I have come to terms with my body.

Jerome Are you a writer, sir?

Powell (*holding up a thick notebook*) The philosophical jottings of a hermit.

Jerome They look pretty substantial.

Powell Going to be a book, one day. An important one, you never know!

Jerome You're a reader, too ...

Powell Have to be! As a schoolmaster before the war, I was too busy to sit down with a book. My martial exploit brought home to me that I was to do nothing but read, and write, for the rest of my life.

As Benjy enters from the kitchen, carrying a tray of crockery etc. for lunch, followed by Madam with a tablecloth

You've stopped feeling sorry for me. (*Turning to go to the veranda, and seeing Benjy*) Who's this?

Benjy Emergency relief, sir, at your service. I was a male nurse, for a spell.

Powell Oh. I suppose that's where I come in.

Benjy Yes, sir. Last thing at night I'm to get your legs off and put you to bed.

Madam (*at the dining-table, setting the tablecloth*) Benjy!

Powell No no, he's down to brass tacks, rather refreshing. (*Turning to go*) I did have a most uncomfortable night ...

Madam You see, Mr Price, our sister's always done it ...

Powell (*to Jerome*) Make yourself at home, you don't mind if I do a little work?

Jerome Of course not, I'll wander round ...

Powell wheels himself on to the veranda, to study notes. Madam examines tumblers, and hands them, one by one, to Benjy, to polish. (NB: No objects should be taken from the tray on to the table, to facilitate the quick change which follows the scene.) Jerome sits on the sofa and takes up a magazine

Cuckoo comes in from the bedroom, nursing Daisy, who is now wrapped in a small quilt. Cuckoo herself is now in a child's straw hat, and has draped gaily coloured paper streamers round her shoulders: she carries a small home-made abacus with white beads

Jerome gets up on her entrance; as she stares at him, and he stares back, he sits again

Cuckoo W-would you like a cup of t-tea?
Jerome (*bewildered*) No thank you.
Madam She can *make* a cup of tea—can't you darling?

Cuckoo sits at the desk, glances at the telephone, plays with the abacus, slides the beads along as she counts, silently and laboriously

(*Busy*) Has she decided who she is today?
Benjy Jus' now, she was Winnie.
Jerome Winnie?
Benjy Winnie Whitechapel, on the wireless, "Funny Ole London" ... (*Going up to her, hands on knees again, as if humouring a child*) 'Ow's Winnie today, ducks?
Cuckoo (*a mechanical but exact dead-pan imitation*) Evah-so-bloomin well Ay-thank-yew ...
Benjy Ain't she a caution?

Madam leaves the dining-table and comes down to the armchair

(*To Cuckoo*) An' Miss Meddle?

Cuckoo does not answer

(*To Jerome*) She's the other one, same programme—(*to Cuckoo*)—Miss Meddle?

No answer

I'm strange, that's what it is ...

Benjy exits to the kitchen

Jerome watches Cuckoo, embarrassed but fascinated. Madam has delved into her bag and starts buffing her nails

Madam She's Lydia's sister.
Jerome Lydia did mention—something ...
Madam You can speak up, she doesn't mind.
Cuckoo (*as Miss Meddle, a ridiculously refined character*) Dew speak up, Ay didn't quate ketch the gist ... (*She closes her eyes*)
Madam Miss *Meddle*! Oh, she has us in stitches sometimes. Quite a bit older than Lydia, of course——
Cuckoo (*Miss Meddle*) A evah so old, old enough to know bettah may deah. (*Opening her eyes, her Welsh accent echoing her mother*) With the child one day old, the nurse dropped her on the floor, dead drunk the nurse was, and the child has been *special* ever since.
Madam She once overheard her mother explaining the facts——
Cuckoo (*still her mother*) A damaged person, that's what the child is.

Jerome looks at her, startled

Madam (*as he does so*) It's all right, she doesn't really know what it means ... Never forgets a thing—do you Cuckoo?

Jerome (*startled*) Cuckoo?

Madam What? ... Oh, it's what we've always called her. A beautiful baby, apparently, then her father was the first to notice—being a doctor, I suppose. Suddenly, one day, he said——

Cuckoo (*sedately*) The child looks c-cuckoo!

Madam (*polishing her nails*) Everybody laughed, and the name stuck. Since then my sister's never left her side, they share that bedroom and last night was the first time they've ever been apart.

Jerome She can't have slept much ...

Madam It wasn't too bad—Lydia moved in, into Mam's bed—thank God!

Powell wheels himself in from the veranda

Powell (*crossing*) I need my dictionary, sorry ... (*He wheels himself to the corner of the desk, and picks up a book*)

Cuckoo (*near him*) Sodden wi' whisky Cuckoo's nurse was, *sodden* ...

Powell (*making a note*) Really ...

Their attitude towards each other is completely negative, masking a mutual dislike

Cuckoo (*out of the blue, absently*) Cuckoo never been to London, or the egg-and-spoon race, or up a tree. (*She arranges the paper streamers over her shoulders*)

Jerome (*making an effort*) We're looking very festive!

Madam (*to him*) It's decorations from the Swan, the hotel where you crossed on the ferry. A big party for the Jubilee.

Cuckoo J-Jubilee?

Madam Yes darling, because King George and Queen Mary have been on the throne for twenty-five years.

Cuckoo (*puzzled, on her way to the bedroom*) Does she s-sit on his knee?

Cuckoo exits to the bedroom, taking Daisy the doll

Madam (*calling, as Cuckoo disappears*) No dear, they've got a throne each. *Mamma mia*, life isn't easy ...

Powell (*to Jerome*) While I remember—her mother's always kept from her about my legs, as it were, apparently it would frighten her, so don't mention——

Jerome Of course not. She's like a child of eight ...

Powell A very slow eight. I've always felt guilty about her, mental weakness just exasperates me, it's callous but I can't help it. I only hope she has no idea.

Madam (*going back to her polishing*) Come Powell, she's not the trouble she might be. (*To Jerome*) Mr Price, since you *may* become ... involved in the family, I'll be realistic. In the world of opera, the more romantic the arias on stage, the more down-to-earth we are in the wings. Well—since you could be wondering—I'm told there are far worse cases than our

Cuckoo—cases not even house-trained—and from the start, that was the one thing her mother was strict about. The dear child *must* have a complex about it, every night is bath night, *basta* . . .

Benjy stands at the kitchen door

Benjy Excuse me Madarm—I am about to chop the meat, would you care to do the potatoes? (*He goes back into the kitchen*)

Madam I have done many things in my life, but never a potato. (*Rising*) We try anything once—*avanti*! (*At the kitchen door, she remembers something, and bursts out laughing*)

Jerome What is it?

Madam The Queen on the King's knee for twenty-five years . . .

She goes into the kitchen

The telephone rings, on the desk. From where he is, Powell can reach it

As he does so, Cuckoo stumbles in from the bedroom, hatless and holding Daisy, and a hair-ribbon, already knotted. She stands at the desk, looking fixedly down at the telephone, afraid to touch it

Powell has taken off the receiver. Jerome watches

Powell (*into the telephone*) Mam! . . . She's here. . . .

He holds the receiver out to Cuckoo, who takes it fearfully and holds to her ear, upside down

Cuckoo Cuckoo . . . c-can't hear . . .

Powell Other way up. (*Impatiently*) No no . . . (*Turning the receiver for her*)

Cuckoo (*listening, bewildered, then with a frantic cry*) Mam! (*To Powell, after a frantic effort*) I can't . . . s-speak . . .

Powell Say hello!

Cuckoo (*into the telephone, desperately*) H . . . H . . .

She looks down at the receiver, lost. Powell takes it from her

Powell (*into the telephone*) She's all right dear—more important, how are *you*? . . . Good, you did give us a turn at breakfast yesterday. . . . Good, Lydia's on her way home, is she? . . . No no, don't worry, everything in hand, lunch? On the way, *don't worry*! . . . What? (*Calling, towards the kitchen*) Did the laundry call?

Madam (*off, from the kitchen*) No idea . . .

Benjy (*off, from the kitchen*) Yeah, I think so . . .

Powell (*into the telephone*) No idea, yeah I think so . . .

Jerome I'll find out.

He hurries into the kitchen

Powell and Cuckoo are alone

Powell (*into the telephone*) Cuckoo? Lost without you, but then we all are. . . . Oh yes, a sort of male nurse who'll see to me, rough but ready, God knows where he came from, and possibly the Labour Exchange—but it's

only till Monday week, that's the date you're due home, isn't it? I'll just
have to shut my eyes and pretend it's you—goodbye dear.... (*He replaces
the receiver*)

Cuckoo Mam far off ...

*Powell picks up his dictionary, and studies it. Cuckoo sees a book on the desk,
takes it, sits on the sofa, and opens the book*

Powell (*looking at her, amused*) What are *you* doing with a book?

*Cuckoo does not answer. Powell turns a page; Cuckoo imitates him, and turns
a page. Irritated, Powell wheels himself towards the veranda*

Lydia (*off, in the garden, to the* L, *hailing*) Cuck-*oo*! (*It is the family cry*)

Cuckoo (*rising, excited, answering the cry*) Cuck-*oo*! Mam's back, Mam's
back—Cuck-*oo*!

*Lydia enters from the veranda. She is in her late twenties, simply dressed,
and carries two books: pretty, attractive and intelligent, with the same direct
simplicity as Jerome. At the moment she is a little jaded, and preoccupied*

Lydia No, love, I'm not Mam–(*laughing*)—I'm Liddy!

*She embraces Cuckoo, with the warm easy affection bestowed on a family pet.
She clips the hair-ribbon into Cuckoo's hair and goes to Powell*

They seem pleased with her, she's in good hands ... (*She kisses the top of
his head*)

Powell I just talked to her—fussed to death about all of us, of course ...

Lydia Of course. (*Placing the two books before him*) I popped into a
bookshop in Kingston and they had both the Thomas Hardys.

Powell Oh thank you my darling, thoughtful of you ...

Lydia (*to Cuckoo*) How's Daisy?

Cuckoo S-splitting headache.

Lydia Too bad—(*to Powell*)—and Madam?

Powell Peeling a potato.

Lydia (*sitting back in the armchair*) I don't believe it. Ah ...

A sentimental waltz approaches, faintly at first, from a punt

Cuckoo Is Cuckoo lost?

Lydia Lost?

Cuckoo Uncle Powell said.

Jerome comes in from the kitchen

Lydia does not see him. The music is louder

Lydia He meant you miss Mam—if Cuckoo *was* lost, we'd all be crying—
(*pretending to cry*)—where's our Cuckoo, mmm ... Where's our
Cuckoo ...

Cuckoo laughs, delighted

Jerome The laundry has not yet called.

Lydia starts on hearing his voice, and turns slowly round to look at him. The music is close by

Powell A punt is passing, loaded with the right mechanical accompaniment. (*To Cuckoo*) Why not give Daisy some fresh air, make her head better?

Cuckoo looks at him impassively, lumbers to her feet and makes her way carefully to the veranda and the garden

Watch me retire on tiptoe. (*Wheeling*) In a manner of speaking.

He goes to his room

Lydia and Jerome are alone. The music begins to die away. She is completely disconcerted by his arrival, and wary of showing any inner excitement; his manner is simple and engaging, but he—in his turn—is controlling an inner tension. He has no idea how she is going to react

Jerome I once asked you why you never ask questions. You said "Because it shows weakness". Is that why you won't ask me why I'm here?

Lydia Did I say that?

Jerome I remember everything you've ever said to me. Ever since six weeks ago last Tuesday, five thirty-one p.m. in a Tube lift.

Lydia You've never talked like this before.

Jerome Lying awake early this morning, I thought it was time I did. I found myself wondering if you were awake too.

Lydia (*carefully*) I overslept.

Jerome Oh ... (*Stepping nearer her*) In the Tube, you were wearing your other dress, with the bow, and a bandage on your little finger, and I'm not naturally observant.

Lydia I remember, I'd cut it sharpening pencils.

Jerome You should have got the office-boy to sharpen them for you.

Lydia I suppose I should ...

Jerome (*after a pause*) All right, small talk ... Miss Roberts, do you *enjoy* office-work?

Lydia It's not unpleasant, Mr Price.

Jerome (*with a twinkle*) The heady scent of carbon-paper, the rapier wit of the very same office-boy as he infuses the tea. You forget I work in an office too ... *I'll* ask *you* a question. Why did you ignore my two notes?

Lydia Because ... (*Rising, and facing him*) Because they were asking me to have dinner with you.

Jerome The second was *begging* you to have dinner with me. And we'd had lunch together in Lyons' Corner House, every other day!

Lydia You know, as well as I do, that in our case dinner would not have been the same. And I shirked writing to say ... "no". (*Looking into his face*) I once had an unhappy love affair.

Jerome (*after a beat*) I guessed that, somehow ...

Lydia (*away from him*) Why walk into trouble when trouble's waiting to walk into you——

Jerome I want you to marry me.

She looks at him, startled: he kisses her, firmly and with fire. They look at each other; at last they know where they are. Lydia sways, as if bewildered

Are you all right?

Lydia A bit ... dazed. (*As he seats her in the armchair*) Did that really happen?

Jerome I'm not sure either ...

He sits on the arm of the chair and takes her hand. The haze of mutual well-being melts, gradually, into a look at the future

Lydia The reason I overslept was because I'd been awake till three. Talking to you.

Jerome Any questions?

Lydia Mostly questions.

Jerome Such as?

Lydia Whether you'd thought of kissing me.

Jerome Next time, you can skip that one.

Lydia What your prospects are.

Jerome (*smiling*) You sound like a Victorian father!

Lydia I do, don't I ...

Jerome My prospects are ... steady.

Lydia Good.

Jerome Good ... enough?

Lydia Ye-es ...

Jerome What d'you mean—ye-es? (*Taking her intonation*)

Lydia My father was a lovely man, but not a particularly good doctor. He died when I was nine, and ever since I've been conscious of being ... poor. So it would be wonderful if you had property instead of prospects.

Jerome I do see.

Lydia But it may not matter, because I practically *know* I'd be happy with you.

Jerome Practically?

Lydia Ninety-five per cent.

Jerome Where do I lose the five?

Lydia On the prospects.

Jerome I see.

Lydia May I think it over?

Jerome Certainly. You'll let me know of any nibbles from any other quarter.

Lydia Certainly.

Jerome Thank you.

Cuckoo (*off, from the garden, singing absently, as before*) "Funny ole London, Jolly ole town ..."

Lydia (*starting up, worried*) Cuckoo ...

She hurries to the veranda door, and peers over the garden. Jerome joins her, his hand on her arm

She's all right, Mam's always afraid she'll fall in. Doesn't she look extraordinary ...

Jerome Sitting like a statue ...

Lydia (*calling, the family cry*) Cuck-oo!

Cuckoo (*off, down the garden*) Cuck-oo!

Jerome What was she staring at?

Lydia The other side of the river—the gate next the school. Where Mam always gets into the dinghy. (*Coming back into the room*) Monday week's a long way off . . .

Madam comes in from the kitchen

Madam I have scraped three potatoes. I have never seen them without their jackets, they look enchanting. *Assez de travail . . .* (*Sitting on the sofa, and seeing Lydia*) Liddy, you're home—how is she?
Lydia Doing well, in good hands . . .
Madam *Maraviglioso . . .*

Benjy stands in the kitchen doorway, as Cuckoo wanders in from the veranda

Benjy (*to Lydia*) Excuse me miss, the laundry.
Lydia Coming . . . (*She checks the tray on the dining-table*)

Benjy goes back into the kitchen

Cuckoo (*to Madam*) Japan.
Madam *Not* the Maid of Japan, *cara*, you're sick of it . . .
Cuckoo Japan!
Jerome Who's the Maid of Japan?

Cuckoo runs up to the fireplace and takes up the dinner-gong and an ornamental bowl with a box of matches in it. She places the bowl in Madam's lap, and hands the gong to Jerome. Lydia walks to the kitchen door

Madam An operetta in which I played the leading role.
Lydia Mam said you were in the chorus.

She goes into the kitchen

Madam A libel—the matches, bravo . . .

She is still on the sofa; Cuckoo lumbers to the desk, picks up a stray envelope, hurries over, skewers it on to a fork from the dining-table, and hands it to Madam. She then squats on the floor at Madam's feet, after taking the bowl from Madam. This is clearly an established routine

(*To Jerome*) Just bang, *caro*, when I give the cue . . .

(*Recitative*) Give to me his love letters . . .

She nods to Jerome; he bangs the gong

My name is Chelly-Blossom . . .

She nods to Jerome; he bangs the gong; she lights a match and applies it to the paper, letting the ash drop into the bowl. As she sings the following, Jerome, who is enjoying himself, bangs the gong after each line, twice, and saying "Pom-Pom" loudly

I am the Maid of Japan—
Who was betrayed by a Man,
His love-letters I burn
As his Passion I spurn . . .

Cuckoo (*singing, shrilly*) Before the Altar of the Gods——

The gong is banged

Madam `⎫`
Jerome `⎭` (*singing*)   Before the Altar of the Gods!

The gong is banged

> *Benjy comes in from the kitchen, stares at the proceedings, and searches for something at the desk*

Madam Now the chorus

(*Singing*)   In old Japan——

Benjy Excuse me, anybody seed a envelope near the phone?
Madam We just burnt it.

Cuckoo holds out the bowl with the charred ashes

Benjy *Burnt* it?
Madam I was the Maid of Japan. It was just an envelope . . .
Benjy Miss Lydia left it this mornin' for the baker. 'E's callin' for it at twelve.
Jerome The baker?
Benjy It 'ad two pound-notes in it.

Madam stares at Benjy

> *Lydia comes in from the kitchen*

Cuckoo puts away the bowl, etc.

Lydia Benjy, did you find it?
Benjy Madam's burnt it.
Lydia She's *what*?
Madam I was being the Maid of Japan.
Lydia But Mam left it yesterday, to pay the baker!
Madam (*contrite*) *Carissima*, what can I say?

> *Powell wheels himself in, from his bedroom*

Cuckoo settles into the armchair

Lydia Madam's burnt two pound-notes.
Powell *What*?

Cuckoo suddenly peals with laughter. The others look at her. Madam bursts into laughter

Madam She's right, it's *molto comico*! I haven't a brass farthing, *but* I've got money to *burn*!

The others are amused, but not Lydia

Look at me, the oldest Geisha on the island—*look* at me! Ha ha . . .

Benjy starts to go

Lydia No—NO!

The others look at her startled

It's no laughing matter!

As Cuckoo gurgles again . . .

Stop, Cuckoo, stop

Cuckoo looks at her round-eyed, hand over mouth

Madam But Liddy, we have always been able to laugh——
Lydia I can't any more—Mam, who put that money by to pay a bill—I can't laugh, I can't . . .

As Jerome steps forward

(*Seeing him*) I forgot you were there. (*She turns, to go into the kitchen*)
Jerome Don't go . . . I have an announcement to make. (*He beats the gong, which he is still holding*)

The others stare at him

Powell (*after a pause*) I know . . . We've no doubt you've got no money either but Lydia's said yes and we congratulate you.
Jerome Correct, except on one point. Perhaps I should have mentioned it before, I shirked it. I—have some money.
Madam (*after a look at Powell*) Would it be vulgar to ask . . . how much?
Powell Of course it would . . . How much!
Jerome My father's in business. You recollect my surname?
Powell A Welsh name—Price . . .
Lydia Price the stationer, Kingston?
Jerome Price and Son, Oxford Street, London.
Benjy *The* Price an' Son?
Jerome *The* Price an' Son. (*Lamely*) I should have told you before.
Madam Are you the Son, capital S?
Jerome Only son, my father retires next year and knows about Lydia.
Benjy (*awed*) It's got seven floors, I counted 'em off the bus——
Jerome And as many branches as a tree. Branches in Liverpool, Birmingham, Coventry——
Powell (*his eyes closed*) Oh what a glorious tree . . .
Madam How much . . . how much have you?
Cuckoo (*bored, rising*) He's got a m-million thruppenny bits.
Benjy Hush, ducks . . .

Cuckoo wanders out on to the veranda and into the garden. A punt approaches, the gramophone playing an infectious happy tune

Madam How much?
Jerome (*crossing, to Lydia*) Well, my father's not Rockefeller, but . . . To be thoroughly vulgar, I'm rich.
Lydia (*bewildered*) But you told me you work in an office!

Jerome I do, quite hard, but I happen to run it as well as work in it. It is possible, my darling, to do both. (*Kissing her, lightly*)

Madam But you travel by Tube!

Jerome I'm a modest man. And rich.

Madam (*after a pause, letting herself go at last*) I *knew* something wonderful would happen to me, it always has!

As the punt passes, the music becomes louder

Jerome Open up the joint for festive water-music! Benjy, unpack my luggage, I brought a bottle, just in case ...

As Benjy takes up the parcel

This little do, ladies and gents is to turn into a celebration!

Benjy hurries into the kitchen. The music gradually dies away

Madam Watch out, I may break into an aria ... Powell, *say* something!

Powell I feel like our great-uncle Caradoc in the pulpit, coming round the bend for the last lap. (*Imitating a dramatical Welsh revivalist preacher*) Oh what a glorious majestic blossoming *tree*! Bless the branch of Liverpool, and of Birmingham, and of Coventry——

Madam (*intoning*) Bless them all!

Powell (*warming to it*) Bless the golden bonuses showering from every bough—bless the gilt-edged stocks and the blooming shares—the budding assets and the sweet-smelling dividends——

Madam (*with Jerome joining in*) Hall-eluyah!

Powell Lydia Roberts—*speech*!

Lydia I—(*faltering*)—I don't know ...

Jerome What's worrying you?

Lydia I was ninety-five per cent sure.

Jerome I remember ...

Lydia I ducked the five per cent.

Jerome Five per cent of salt in a good dish is *just right*—I love that five per cent!

Benjy returns from the kitchen, with—on a tray—an opened bottle of champagne and five tumblers. He pours and distributes the tumblers

Madam To *Lydia*! (*Rising, raising her champagne, and bursting into song—a joyous operatic burst of Italian thanksgiving*) Grazie al Cielo ... Per questo Miracolo. ... Grazie a Dio...

She repeats the phrases, as the others join in, in improvised harmony

(*A sudden happy idea*) Let's ring the hospital! (*Moving round the sofa*)

Powell Yes, let's ...

Lydia (*going to the telephone*) I still can't believe it ...

Madam *Mamma mia*—what will she *say*?

Lydia (*looking for the number on a pad*) "All that money", she'll say, "it doesn't seem right——"

The telephone rings

Oh bother ... (*Lifting the receiver*) Yes? ... It's the hospital—Mam!
Madam Telepathy! Let me talk to her too ... (*Humming*)
Lydia (*into the telephone*) Oh?
Powell What is it?
Lydia They're putting me through to Matron.
Powell The Matron?

Madam stops humming

Madam How tiresome of her, we want Mam ...
Lydia (*into the telephone*) Matron ...

On the river, a punt approaches, playing a feverishly jolly tune, quietly at first

How do you mean, more serious?

Cuckoo lumbers in from the veranda

Cuckoo (*seeing the telephone, eagerly*) Telly-phony?
Powell ⎱
Madam ⎰ (*together*) Serious?
Lydia (*into the telephone*) Yes, I'll be there ...
Jerome I'll drive you ...

Lydia replaces the receiver, slowly

Cuckoo (*disappointed*) Oh ... (*She sits on the stool, her back to the audience, her head disconsolately bent, she has taken in nothing of the situation. But she is suddenly the centre of the group*)
Powell How serious?
Lydia They'll know more after tomorrow morning.

They look at each other, as the Lights fade: for a second, a spotlight lingers on Cuckoo's back, then fades into darkness as the CURTAIN *falls and the music swells. The* CURTAIN *rises again as soon as possible, on:*

SCENE 2

Five weeks later; an afternoon in July. Mellow sunlight

Daisy the doll is again sitting upright on the stool, but she is now in black: a clumsily sewn shift. A different plant, near the dresser. There are signs of upheaval. On the small table, a large tea-chest, half-full of stuff to be thrown away. On the floor between desk and sofa, two separate piles of family albums, letters, cuttings, diaries etc.; a third unsorted pile. The bedroom and kitchen doors are again open

Jerome stands at the telephone, hanging on. He wears an open sports shirt and a sweater. A pause

Benjy enters from the corridor, from L. He is in shirt-sleeves, and wears a worn-out green-baize apron. He carries a pile of old newspapers and other debris from any house-moving from a settled home, such as a battered old waste-paper basket. He pitches the load into the tea-chest, and goes to the kitchen

Jerome (*into the telephone*) Furniture removers? ... This is Mr Price, of Price and Son ...

As he hangs on, Benjy stops at the kitchen door and laughs uncontrollably to himself

After five weeks, haven't you got over the funny side of my money *yet*?
Benjy Sorry sir, it's them seven floors in Oxford Street ...

He goes into the kitchen, leaving the door open

Jerome (*into the telephone*) I want to check about the day after tomorrow. ... No, not from the Swan, that's where I'm staying. ... No, the Kozy Kot job. ...

Lydia enters from the corridor, from L; she wears a new dress, unobtrusively smart. She carries a chipped jug with a broken handle, and a torn lampshade. She kneels above the piles of objects to be sorted, and stuffs the jug and the lampshades into the waste-paper basket near her. She continues to sort

(*Into the telephone*) That's it. ... So will you have the van backed into School Lane opposite, on to the river, nine a.m. sharp. Right, goodbye. ... (*Replacing the receiver*) There'll be a man at the London flat to help you move in.
Lydia Thank you ... After five weeks of saying "thank you", I'm becoming a bore.

The telephone rings. Jerome answers it

Jerome Emberbrook oh-three-four-seven. ... Ah ... (*To Lydia*) My secretary ... (*Into the telephone*) Yes? ... Good—and we sail from Tilbury? ... (*Sitting at the desk and scribbling*) Marseilles. ... Genoa twelfth. ... Rome fifteenth—any message from my father? ... Oh, would you read it? "Enjoyed lunch with you both", yes. ... "Congratulations", thank you. (*Replacing the receiver*) He likes you.
Lydia I like him.
Jerome Every *been* to sea?
Lydia Twice. At Bognor, in my depth.
Jerome You're going to sea, out of your depth.
Lydia I know ...

Jerome moves from the desk, as she suddenly notices a snapshot, and sits looking at it

Jerome What's that one of?
Lydia That's me. On her knee.

Upset, she puts her hand up to her face. Jerome sits on the sofa and takes her in his arms

   I won't do that again.
Jerome Try not to.

He is about to kiss her, when they hear a noise of crockery in the kitchen. They look in that direction, and separate

   Cuckoo enters from the kitchen, carrying a plate piled with small pieces of bread. She is bare-headed

Jerome goes to the dining-table, sits, and addresses travel labels. Lydia picks up her papers, and sits at the desk, to sort them out

Lydia What have you got there, darling?
Cuckoo T-tea-time, for the swans.
Lydia Mind the sofa.

   Cuckoo just manages to avoid the sofa. Then she looks around, espies Daisy on the stool, goes down to her, takes her carefully up, and walks carefully to the veranda and on to the garden

Lydia continues to sort; Jerome continues with his labels

   Benjy comes in from the kitchen, holding out a battered suitcase, lid open

Benjy This do, sir?
Jerome Good, it'll take a pile of stuff all ready in the lumber-room ...
Benjy Right ...
Lydia And don't forget, we've got somebody special coming to tea.
Benjy Right ... (*Going up to the archway*)
Lydia And Madam should be here any minute ...
Benjy Right ...
Jerome Benjy, where do *you* go from here?
Benjy Pay me respects. (*He starts to go*)
Jerome Girl-friend?
Benjy Labour Exchange. " 'Ere 'e comes", they'll say, "ole faithful! Dig the garden, mind the baby, comfort the wife, all in the day's work, I thank yew!"

   He goes off to L, with the suitcase

Jerome (*writing*) I'm looking forward to seeing Madam, after three weeks gallivanting in the wicked city.
Lydia The Savoy Hotel—you shouldn't have done it ... Oh, she rang yesterday, she'd been to vet the St John's Wood flat, it'll be ready for her in three weeks. Ah ... (*She finishes sorting*)
Jerome Did she approve?
Lydia Not as grand as she'd like, I could tell, but she *is* thrilled. I've warned you of the money she's been through in her time, I can't do more ...
Madam (*off, at the back door*) Cuck-*oo*!
Lydia (*rising, answering the cry*) Cuck-*oo*!

Jerome also rises

Madam sails in from the kitchen. She is dressed to kill, in elegant suit and hat, the elegance marred by too many ruffles and accessories; she carries an overnight bag, and is at the top of her Italianate form

Madam (*singing, joyously*) *Grazie al Cielo. Per questo Miracolo!* (*Embracing Lydia, then Jerome*) *Carissima famiglia mia* . . .
Jerome The car picked you up all right? (*Taking her case and putting it down*)
Madam A Daimler my dear, deposited me at the Swan and if humanly possible would have driven across the river and down the path to the old back door! (*Sitting, on the sofa*) My dears, Madam feels *molto expensiva!*
Lydia (*going to the desk*) An expensive diva! (*Starting to sort books, from the bookshelves*)
Madam Exactly. *Bellissimo* Jerome, I've gone through all my pin-money.
Lydia Madam, you *promised* . . .
Madam It was the Salon de Beauté, face, hair, nails, I had everything, *scusi.*
Jerome *Prego.*
Lydia Your old room's ready for you. A bit bare, I'm afraid with all the packing . . .
Madam My old room . . . (*Looking around, sobering*) The old place. (*Sincerely sad*) I cried for three days, didn't I darling—then I said to myself, child . . . if you don't rise above, you'll go under, law of gravity. . .

Jerome has sat again at the dining-table, to finish the labels

Jerome Quite right—I'll never forget you at the funeral, in white.
Lydia You know it outraged the neighbours?
Madam It was meant to.

Benjy enters, from the archway, from L, *carrying the loaded suitcase*

Jerome Hickidoola on the left, Nest O' Robinsons on the right.
Madam *Buon giorno*, Benjy!
Benjy (*with a bow*) Welcome 'ome, Madarm.
Madam Ah . . .

Benjy goes into the kitchen

And Powell?
Lydia A bit of a problem.
Madam Oh? Is Benjy not working out?
Jerome Oh, Benjy's fine, puts him to bed like a baby, they're pals . . .
Madam Then what is the problem?
Lydia He just never comes out of that room . . .
Jerome And now we've got a good excuse to *get* him out—(*going up to the archway and disappearing to* R *then calling*)—Uncle Powell! (*He comes back*)
Lydia (*calling*) Madam's here! (*To Madam*) It'll do him good to see you . . .

Powell wheels himself into the room. He has changed, visibly, looks ill and listless, and has lost his pride in his appearance. The tray before him is without books or papers

Powell What is it?

Madam Powell *caro*, it's me!
Powell Oh ... Yes—sorry dear—(*with an effort*)—good ...
Lydia Do you want some books fetched?
Powell (*shielding his eyes*) Don't bother.
Lydia It's so dark in your room in the mornings, and it's lovely on the
    veranda ...
Jerome I'll wheel you out——
Powell (*coldly*) I can manage. (*He moves towards the veranda*)
Jerome Uncle Powell, about the day after tomorrow. There's a car coming
    for you at ten——
Powell I can't get into a car, what d'you mean? (*Wheeling round at him*)
Jerome It's ... it's an ambulance.
Powell Ambulance?
Jerome It's the only size for the chair.
Powell And where does it take me, hospital?
Lydia Jerome told you—we've taken a ground-floor flat for you and me.
Jerome In Chelsea, with a garden——
Lydia Until I'm married, then you can decide what you want to do.
Jerome By then you might feel like going off on a boat somewhere——
Madam You're always talking about the Parthenon, now you can *see* it!
Powell (*after a pause*) No thank you. I've become such a creature of habit it
    might affect my health.

*He wheels himself on to the veranda. A punt has been approaching, with a
gramophone playing jazz*

Lydia He says he sleeps, but he doesn't.
Madam He's still writing his book, though?
Lydia (*back at sorting books*) Writing? He's not even reading.
Madam That's bad, *cara*, isn't it?

The music is louder. Powell swivels his chair, violently and re-enters

Powell Those damn gramophones—and this morning that blasted council
    school over the way, children pouring out like a lot of parakeets——

As Jerome makes to help him

    I can manage, thank you!

    He propels himself to his room. The music dies away

Lydia So long as he doesn't start drinking ...
Jerome But has he, in the past?
Madam *Si si*—after his war accident, you know, the land-mine—he had a
    terrible bout, then *presto*, he went on the wagon and stayed on it ...
Jerome Oh Lord ...
Lydia What is it?
Jerome Yesterday he sent Benjy over to the Swan for a bottle of whisky.
Lydia Oh.
Jerome And Cuckoo?

Jerome turns his head and looks at Lydia. A pause. He rises

We've been avoiding the subject, for days.

Lydia (*leaning against the desk, arms folded*) Cuckoo ... I haven't the faintest idea about.

Madam After I left—did she ever sense the fact there had been a funeral?

Jerome We just don't know.

Madam Liddy, *how* you coped with that, so splendid——

Lydia Wasn't it awful? Pretending to her it was a birthday party for you, and not a wake, ghastly ... (*She paces*)

Madam But ... didn't you tell me on the phone that she has dressed her doll in *black*?

Lydia She has. When I asked her why, she said, everybody in black except Madam, so Daisy can't be left out.

Jerome And where does that take us?

Madam But *cara*, you had to break it to her in the end?

Lydia I tried to. And as I started, I realized that though I've known her all my life, I've never had the most elementary conversation with her. I know Benjy much better.

Madam How did you put it?

Lydia I said, "Mam's gone on a journey".

Madam And?

Lydia She looked me straight in the face and said, "When is she coming back?" Those steady beautiful eyes, like a ... like a dog trying to understand, it broke my heart. And I said, "I don't know ..." I just ducked it.

Madam But she realizes you're getting married?

Lydia I've ducked that too.

Jerome (*sitting again at the dining-table*) And how she'll react to the move is anybody's guess. All I know is that this is the second time I'm writing labels for the furniture. The first time ... they just disappeared.

Lydia I'm sure she'll love the London flat, and the garden, I'll tell her it's a holiday ...

Madam And after that?

Jerome After that ...

Lydia That's why we sent for you.

Madam I wondered why ... But where do I come in?

Lydia Through Mam's will.

Madam Oh?

Jerome Which states, "I entrust the care of my elder daughter to my younger daughter Lydia and to my only sister, knowing they will decide the best course to take".

Madam She wants *me* to be responsible?

Lydia She does.

Madam All those years, my darling sister refused to realize how silly I am! Ah well ... "The best course to take" ... I suppose poor Cuckoo will have to go into a—*come si chiama*—a home?

Lydia (*sharply*) No!

Madam Oh?

Lydia Our Cuckoo surrounded by strangers, all of them ... with something the matter—oh, we've gone into it——

Madam But it's the obvious way out——

Lydia Madam darling, can you *imagine* Mam being told Cuckoo's ending up in a *home*? The look on her face?

Madam I see what you mean ...

Jerome It would haunt you for the rest of your lives.

Lydia paces again

Madam (*as she does so*) Then what will happen?

Lydia It'll depend on the ...

Jerome The ... What the hell did we decide to call her?

Madam Who?

Lydia The woman for her.

Madam The woman for her—*cara*, what do you mean?

Lydia "Nurse" is such a depressing word——

Jerome I remember—"companion".

Lydia Of course. Oh, we've combed every agency in London. (*Taking a paper from the desk*) These were the finalists. (*She hands it to Madam*)

Madam (*reading, extending her arm*) "Whittaker. Nice woman, more than possible."

Lydia Going to New York in six weeks, to get married.

Madam (*reading*) "Mason". You've written "jolly face".

Lydia She drinks.

Jerome Jolly faces often do.

Madam (*reading*) "Milford. Jolly face ... teetotaller"! Well?

Lydia Er ... now what was the snag ...

Jerome Stone deaf.

Madam (*reading*) "Swinley. Intense but sympathetic."

Jerome Turned out to be a novelist.

Lydia She'd have stayed a week and spent a year writing about us.

Madam (*reading*) "Dix".

Lydia She's the one we've decided on. Mrs Dix.

Madam What is she like?

Lydia Hard to describe.

Jerome Not a ball of fire, but ...

Lydia Very ... nice. And intelligent. She's a graduate of the Palmer Institute of Psychiatry, in Kingsway.

Benjy comes in from the kitchen, with a tray of cups and saucers, etc., and places the tray on the desk

She's the one who's coming to tea—thank you Benjy.

Benjy bows and goes back into the kitchen

She seems very sensible. I have a good feeling about her.

Madam She sounds all right! So——

She stops, much as Lydia and Jerome did before, as ...

Cuckoo approaches, on the veranda with the plate and her doll, and comes into the room. Cuckoo does not look at her, as she leaves the plate on the dining-room table and crosses them on her way to the bedroom

Lydia Did you feed the swans?
Cuckoo B-bread upon the waters.
Lydia Look who's here!
Madam (*her arms out, smiling with the family cry*) Cuck-*oo*!
Cuckoo (*without turning round, distant and solemn, a new act*) Evah so
  'appy, to make your bloomin' acquaintance, evah so bloomin' so.

Madam looks at the others and shrugs

Madam Thank you, Winnie Whitechapel. And how is Miss Meddle?
Cuckoo (*a different voice*) Tolerebbly well, thenking your Leddyship. (*She
  smoothes Daisy's dress and turns towards the bedroom. In doing so she sees
  the telephone, and seems slowly mesmerized by it. She sits in the desk-chair,
  and with immense concentration, lifts her hand towards the receiver*)
Lydia (*an involuntary muffled cry*) No . . .

*Cuckoo has not heard. Lydia looks helplessly at the others. Cuckoo seems to
brace herself, and finally takes up the receiver and slowly, fearfully, puts it to
her ear. She listens, with the same immense concentration, then looks at the
receiver and replaces it. For the first time, we see in her face a look of immense
sorrow, the sorrow of bereavement*

Jerome (*abrupt, loud, measured*) Cuckoo, where is Mam?

*Lydia and Madam look at him in startled apprehension, then back at Cuckoo.
Cuckoo rises, suddenly, spasmodically, and faces them: a startling switch to
bright reasonableness. She is acting again*

Cuckoo Mam's gone on a journey.
Jerome And is she coming back?
Cuckoo Oh yes! B-because she said to C-cuckoo, I'll be back, and Mam
  would never *never* tell a lie. (*Turning her back slowly to them, as she
  approaches the bedroom door*) She'll be back. Just you wait.

  She goes into the bedroom

Lydia, distressed, puts a hand to her face

Madam Oh dear, *what* are we to do . . .

  *Benjy comes in from the kitchen, holding an elaborate tea-stand which has
  seen better days, decorated with bread-and-butter, cakes and accessories.
  He has discarded his apron, and wears a tie. He closes the door*

Madam rises and comes down to examine the tea-stand

Madam *Sapristi*, I have not seen this object since I was thirteen!
Lydia Benjy, where did you find it?
Benjy In the glory-'ole miss. I give it a flick o' me duster. We got a visitor,
  Madarm.
Madam So I hear.

Benjy goes up to the hatstand for his jacket, which he puts on

  The way he calls me Madarm, too *simpatico*. Actually Liddy, give him a
  fierce moustache and he *is* my Count Alber-rto. But *that* is in my buried
  past . . .

As Benjy comes down again, a knock at the kitchen door. Lydia looks at Jerome; he opens the door, as Benjy busies himself with the tea-tray on the desk

Mrs Dix walks in

Lydia Ah, good——
Mrs Dix I plead guilty to barging in via the cuisine, so many pardons ha ha.

She is as Lydia said: hard to describe, but very nice. She is an English matron of indeterminate age, well-bred and well-educated. She has, however, no sense of humour; her intermittent "ha ha" is not a mirthful laugh, merely the mechanical chuckle of one who is keeping the conversation going. Her clothes are sensible, her hat unnoticeable. She carries a handbag and a raincoat

Lydia Mr Price you've met——
Mrs Dix Of course ... (*Looking around, kindly*) What a *dear* little band-box!

Jerome brings forward a chair for Lydia, then takes Mrs Dix's coat and hangs it on the hatstand

Madam (*offended*) R-really? *How* do you do?

Mrs Dix looks at her, then sits on the stool

Mrs Dix (*to Madam*) So *you* are to be my little friend!

Madam stares at her. The others are too much at a loss to say anything

Madam (*crushingly*) I am Madam Ellis, your humble servant of La Scala, Milan.
Mrs Dix Yes dear, of course you are.
Jerome I'm sorry Mrs Dix, but your patient—I mean—the person in question——
Lydia Is *my* sister, this is my mother's sister.
Mrs Dix Oh crumbs ... (*To Madam, who is looking beyond approach*) What a laughable mistake, ha ha ...
Madam Side-splitting.
Mrs Dix I'm afraid when you made your joke about being Madam Ellis——
Madam (*more crushing*) I am Madam Ellis!
Mrs Dix (*looking at her, then realizing*) Of *course* you are—I recognize you from the photograph!
Madam (*almost mollified*) Ah ...
Mrs Dix Mother adored opera, collected *everybody*!
Madam (*withering again*) *Grazie.*

Benjy pours tea, Jerome dispenses it

Lydia (*to Mrs Dix*) Did you have a good journey?
Mrs Dix Umpteen changes doncher know, Box and Cox the order of the day, but I'm a martyr to conversations in trains. They teach you *so* much, Queen Eavesdrop that's me, ha ha ... I'm as happy as a sandboy!

Jerome (*to her*) Milk, sugar?

Mrs Dix Just the cow-juice, ta ever so . . .

Madam (*her Italian accent to the fore*) How happy *eez* a sandboy?

Lydia Madam——

Mrs Dix (*unabashed, helpful*) It's an English figure of speech, Madam Ellis.

Madam (*losing the point*) Thank you. (*Rising*) I think I'll have my tea *al fresco*. (*Going towards the veranda*) Ciao!

Jerome (*to Mrs Dix*) Cake?

Mrs Dix Oh, scrumptious . . . Madam Ellis, La Scala Milan must have been out of this world!

Benjy goes towards the kitchen door

Madam Very much *in*, it was my job. (*Calling*) Wasn't it, Benjy?

Benjy (*startled*) Was it, Madarm?

Mrs Dix (*puzzled*) You worked for Madam Ellis, at La Scala?

Madam He dressed me.

She goes out on to the veranda with her tea, and disappears into the garden

Mrs Dix (*her eyes widening, Benjy's too*) Crumbs . . .

An awkward pause, though not awkward for her

Jerome Mrs Dix, about your work—you've had a great deal of experience of this sort of thing?

Mrs Dix Indeed yes. (*To Lydia*) After taking my degree in Psychology—as a girl, I fear, I was a teensy bit of a blue-stocking—I plunged into Psychiatry and Psychiatric Therapy doncher know, in relation to interesting cases. Since my divorce—an alcoholic poor dear—I've devoted myself to what I call oddies.

Lydia Oddies?

Mrs Dix Oddies! To me, half the trouble in coping with the retarded is the lack of a cozy name for them. Simpletons, cretins, loonies, all *horrid* words, so I hit on "oddies". Good isn't it—ha ha . . .

Jerome It sounds a silly question—Mrs Dix, are you fond of children?

Mrs Dix Not silly at all, you *are* engaging a sort of nanny! To me, my charges are foster-babies, poor dears.

Lydia Good . . .

Jerome And who was your last . . . oddie?

Mrs Dix I was for seven years with Lady Ruth Pillie. (*Social*) She lived with her brother, Lord William. She was Ruth to me, naturally.

Lydia Oh yes?

Mrs Dix Backward, but the pet of the world. Lord William had that amazing collection of china. She couldn't be allowed near it, of course. (*Sipping*)

Jerome Of course. She died?

Mrs Dix No, went to Australia. Lord William is Lieutenant-General there, since when I've been Ruthless, ha ha . . . Is she troublesome?

Lydia Oh . . . No no, she's never been any trouble to us.

Mrs Dix Spoilt, of course?

Lydia (*disconcerted, looking at Jerome*) Well . . . Her mother——

Mrs Dix Oh, it's impossible for an oddie brought up at home to be anything else. Have you always conversed with her in baby-talk?

Lydia Baby-talk? I suppose we have . . .

Mrs Dix Oh it's common, Mummy starts and it goes on—not a criticism, just that it encourages them to stay childish . . . Now! (*Rising, walking and putting her hands together, the brisk professional*) I votes that Cuckoo and I—priceless name, such fun, ha ha—I votes that we establish a relationship, as our American cousins put it. Without telling her the plan until she's used to me. (*Sitting, again*)

Jerome (*to Lydia*) Carried?

Lydia Carried.

They both rise

Mrs Dix So far so good.

Jerome goes to the bedroom door

Jerome (*calling*) Cuckoo . . .

Mrs Dix I'll go carefully.

> *Benjy comes in from the kitchen, carrying a jug of hot water; he goes to the desk to pour into the teapot*

> *Cuckoo wanders in from the bedroom, the quilt over her arm. She is wearing a different hat, a pill-box. She wanders forward, as Benjy makes for the kitchen door*

Lydia Darling, I want you to meet somebody.

Cuckoo (*pointing suddenly at Benjy*) Cuckoo *met* him . . .

He turns round and faces her, nervously. She walks on

> (*Amiably*) God knows where he came from, and possibly the Labour Exchange.

> *Benjy retreats into the kitchen*

Jerome No Cuckoo, this is somebody new.

Lydia Who would like to be your friend.

Cuckoo has reached the armchair. Mrs Dix rises

> This is Mrs Dix.

Slowly, Cuckoo turns and looks at the newcomer. Her steady blank expression would disconcert most people, but not Mrs Dix

Mrs Dix Dixie to her friends!

> *Madam returns from the veranda, and hands her cup to Jerome*

Cuckoo (*sitting, suddenly, in the armchair, and singing*) "Take me back to dear old Dixie, jolly old Dixieland . . ."

Mrs Dix That was *very* nice.

Cuckoo Now *you* sing it.
Lydia Cuckoo——
Mrs Dix Of course I will, dear! (*Singing quite unselfconsciously, on the note but unpleasing*) "Take me back to dear old Dixie, jolly old Dixieland!"

Madam, on her way to her room, has turned round to listen

Cuckoo Can you turn a s-somersault?
Mrs Dix No dear.
Madam You surprise me.

She goes into her bedroom, banging the door

Cuckoo draws the quilt round her and seems to fall asleep

Mrs Dix (*to Lydia and Jerome*) Right! (*She sits again, on the stool*)
Lydia You will remember, won't you, that she's never had a stranger talk to her before?
Mrs Dix I will.

As they move towards the kitchen . . .

Oh . . . (*Opening her bag and bringing out a notepad and pencil*) One question I would like answered . . .
Lydia Yes?
Mrs Dix How independent is she?
Lydia Independent?
Mrs Dix Has she been trained to sleep alone?
Lydia I'm afraid not—she's always shared with her mother, that bedroom . . .
Mrs Dix And from the time her mother . . . passed away?
Lydia I moved in there.
Mrs Dix Into your mother's bed?
Lydia Yes.
Mrs Dix (*making a note*) Interesting. Thank you . . .

The others turn to go; Jerome stops, and looks at Lydia

Jerome We haven't put it into words, but . . . she's got us in the palm of her hand.
Mrs Dix Don't *worry*! I'll call you.
Jerome Yes, do. Come along, darling . . .

They go into the kitchen; the door closes behind them

Cuckoo has not moved. Mrs Dix looks at her; a pause

Mrs Dix Cuckoo . . .

No reaction

Cuckoo!
Cuckoo Cuckoo! (*A perfect imitation*)
Mrs Dix (*unperturbed*) Shall I tell you something? Hats don't suit you at all, you're too pretty. Won't you take it off?

Cuckoo (*she has still not moved, her eyes are still shut*) No thank you.

Mrs Dix Cuckoo, why are you behaving like this?

Cuckoo Cuckoo got a pain.

Mrs Dix (*another try*) No you haven't. You've got something on your mind, haven't you?

No reaction

You're sad . . . aren't you?

A pause. It is as if a nerve, in Cuckoo, has been touched. She sits up, with startling suddenness, and sings babyishly, the parody of a jingle

Cuckoo "I gorra be bed bed bed, 'cos I gorra be sed sed sed . . ." (*She lies spasmodically back, pulls the quilt over her head, and stays motionless, like a shrouded corpse*)

Mrs Dix (*patient*) Sit up Cuckoo, and don't be silly.

Cuckoo (*under the quilt*) Sit up Cuckoo, and don't be sillay. (*Again a perfect imitation*)

Mrs Dix, the hundred-per-cent sane kind machine, is, for the moment, jammed. But she is not going to admit defeat. She rises and walks, pondering on her next move. She makes a decision, returns to the small table, takes up her bag and opens it

Mrs Dix Cuckoo, there are precious few things that Dixie doesn't know about you, you'd be surprised! And one of them is . . . Your sister Lydia told me you collect thruppenny bits!

A pause. The quilt is lowered a few inches, uncovering Cuckoo's eyes as they fix on Mrs Dix

Well, I've got something *ten times* the value of a thruppenny bit!

Cuckoo sits up: Mrs Dix is holding out a half-crown piece

Cuckoo (*Winnie Whitechapel*) *Ain't* it enormous ducky . . .

Mrs Dix It's got the *King* on it!

Cuckoo 'Ow much dja want fer eet?

Mrs Dix It's something money can't buy. (*Dropping the coin into her bag and closing it with a snap*)

Cuckoo (*Miss Meddle*) Dixay, *pray* don't be sillay.

Mrs Dix sits again, on the stool

Mrs Dix (*patient*) I'll what I call strike a bargain, dear. I'll give you the King if you'll be a good girl and take that thing off your head and answer my questions. Right?

Cuckoo looks at her a moment, then with a decisive movement whisks off her hat

Question time, we're off!

Cuckoo Animal, vegetable, m-mineral!

Mrs Dix Where d'you want to go most in the world?

Cuckoo (*after quick thought*) Heaven, *and* all over B-Broadcasting House. Then back to Kozy Kot.

Mrs Dix Would you be very upset if you had to *leave* Kozy Kot?

As before the direct question touches a nerve, and Cuckoo evades it

Cuckoo Cuckoo *is* leaving.

Mrs Dix You are? Who told you?

Cuckoo Mam did.

Mrs Dix When did she tell you?

Cuckoo (*faltering*) I c-can't remember. In one ear out the other.

Mrs Dix Where will she take you?

Cuckoo Somewhere utterly nice, Mam said. (*Prattling, anything to avoid the issue*) We'll move, she exclaimed eagerly, Mam always keeps a promise, come rain or come shine, a veritable J-Jibberalter. There'll be a garden, if there anything I like it's a g-garden, in London perhaps. (*Singing, wilfully, as if absentminded*) "Funny ole London, Jolly ole town . . ."

She lies back again, and closes her eyes. Mrs Dix, stymied again, gets up and walks, thoughtfully. She consults her notepad, then turns to Cuckoo

Mrs Dix Next question, animal!

As Cuckoo sits up again, eagerly

What do you want to be, most in the world?

Cuckoo (*after quick thought*) Cuckoo. Cuckoo was dropped on her head one day old and is ab-absolutely unique. Cuckoo is a s-special person.

Mrs Dix Not *quite* unique, dear. I've been dealing with special persons for years, and I know. (*Sitting again, on the stool*)

Cuckoo (*sharply, taken aback*) What s-sort of special persons?

Mrs Dix Lady Ruth Pillie, for instance. (*Social again*) She and I were tremendously pallsy-wallsy.

Cuckoo Was *she* dropped on her head?

Mrs Dix No dear, she was *born* special.

Cuckoo *Born* special? Nobody was ever *born* special, except in the B-Bible. And you were never pallsy-wallsy with any of *them* . . . What did she do, more s-special than Cuckoo?

Mrs Dix She . . . laughed a lot.

Cuckoo How much?

Mrs Dix Most of the time, I'm afraid.

Cuckoo Anybody can do that. (*Anxious*) What else?

Mrs Dix She jumped up and down . . .

Cuckoo Cuckoo do that, only s-skipping. What else?

Mrs Dix She could tell the time . . .

Cuckoo So can Cuckoo, falling off a log. Could she make a cup of tea?

Mrs Dix No. She'd have made rather a mess of the kitchen.

Cuckoo J-Jumping up and down with a teapot, and laughing? She does sound a case. What else?

Mrs Dix sighs, a little discouraged. She rises again, and walks

Mrs Dix Oh . . . (*A sudden idea*) She can read! (*She is pleased to be able to boast about her friend, at last*) Next question——

Cuckoo (*sitting up, stung*) She could read? The right way up?

Mrs Dix Yes——

Cuckoo Cat, mat, further absorbing instalment, please turn to page four for d-details of competition?

Mrs Dix Yes! In between . . . She would curl up and have a jolly good read.

Cuckoo In between l-laughing and jumping up and down?

Mrs Dix Yes——

Cuckoo She could *read* . . . (*This has hurt her: sharply*) How did she m-manage that?

Mrs Dix (*moving back to the stool*) *I* was her teacher! (*Sitting, happily*) So I can teach you to be as clever as Lady Pillie—I can teach *you* to read!

Cuckoo looks at her

Cuckoo (*flatly*) No.

Mrs Dix No? Oh, why not?

Cuckoo Do you *want* to know?

Mrs Dix I do, I'm very curious!

Cuckoo It won't be good news.

Mrs Dix *Why* don't you want me to teach you?

Cuckoo Because . . . (*Hesitating*) Just because. (*Looking away*)

Mrs Dix Oh . . . (*Taking it in her stride*) You mean you don't like me, *I* know . . .

Cuckoo It isn't g-good news, is it?

Mrs Dix Fiddle-dee-dee, you *will* get to like me, just you wait!

Cuckoo Could she read the *Radio Times*?

Mrs Dix From cover to cover! Now—(*looking at her notepad*)—ah—the Big Question . . .

Cuckoo sits back and again pretends to go to sleep. Mrs Dix rises above this, makes a decision, turns towards the kitchen, rises and goes smartly to the kitchen door

(*Calling*) Miss Roberts, Mr Price! (*Back to the stool*)

Lydia (*off, in the kitchen*) Coming!

She comes in from the kitchen, followed by Jerome

Yes?

Mrs Dix (*to them*) I want you to hear this next move . . . (*Sitting again*) It's a sort of game, you see, what I call a psychological gambit, can bring the truth to the surface quite unexpectedly. Now Cuckoo, the Big Question!

Cuckoo opens her eyes, sits up, and looks steadily at Mrs Dix

Now where's my list . . . (*Finding it*) Ah . . . Now . . . Whom do you love most in the world, next to Mam?

Cuckoo D-Daisy.

Mrs Dix Daisy? Not on my list . . . Ah, *dolly*, jolly good! Next? (*Writing, on her list*)

Cuckoo Madam next, lower down.

Mrs Dix Next? Uncle Powell?

Cuckoo Oh no.

Mrs Dix No? Why?

Cuckoo Such a L-Lazybones ... Cuckoo can't run or swim with being s-such a lump, but Cuckoo worship people running and swimming but not Uncle Powell.

Mrs Dix Oh dear ... Next?

Cuckoo The postman—no, he limps, can Cuckoo have the King of the thruppeny bits?

Mrs Dix (*scanning her list*) In a minute dear ...

Cuckoo Silly L-Lady Pillie ...

Mrs Dix But Cuckoo ... (*Carefully*) There's one person you've missed out!

Cuckoo Who?

Mrs Dix looks at the other two, then back at Cuckoo

Your sister Lydia!

A strange look comes over Cuckoo's face: a look of secret concentration on one idea, secret and almost fierce. Slowly, she draws the quilt again over her head and lies inertly back

(*To the others*) Ah ... Now we're getting somewhere. (*She rises*)

Lydia But where?

Mrs Dix This is what I meant about bringing a truth to the surface. This is the moment for the question ... which has never been asked. Cuckoo, is ... Mam——

Lydia (*stepping forward, an involuntary cry*) Don't ask it!

Mrs Dix If you don't mind, Miss Roberts, it's a good move ... Cuckoo, is Mam dead?

A pause. Then from under the quilt, Cuckoo's voice. It is loud, firm aggressive

Cuckoo No!

A pause. With a sudden wild movement, she sits bolt upright, at the same time flinging the quilt on to the floor

Mrs Dix (*gently, but still the psychiatrist*) But where is she?

Cuckoo rises slowly to her feet; she appears to be in a trance, auto-suggested, painfully concentrated. She walks, slowly, towards the kitchen: it is like sleep-walking, weird but not grotesque. She passes Lydia, then turns and looks at her

Cuckoo Mam ...

She sinks to the floor, and clasps Lydia to her: transported, happy. Lydia looks down at her, then at Jerome

The CURTAIN *falls slowly*

ACT II

SCENE 1

The same. Some hours later, near midnight

Before the CURTAIN *rises, in the darkness, light music of the period. As the action begins, the music continues more faintly, on the river*

The lamps are lit. At the near veranda table, Mrs Dix sits, typing busily at Madam's typewriter, stationery and envelopes by her side. The kitchen door is shut. The desk-chair is now below the desk, against the wall. Daisy the doll is sitting upright on the stool, back now in her light-coloured dress. Near the dresser, a tray with a couple of bottles and glasses. Benjy stands at the desk, turning over the pages of a large book of prints. He wears his jacket. Jerome sits on the edge of the armchair, shuffling a pack of cards on the small table

The music dies away; Mrs Dix finishes typing, closes the typewriter, puts it on the floor, and begins to write and address letters. Benjy has come across an engraving which intrigues him; he steps forward and shows it to Jerome

Benjy What's this a pitcher of?
Jerome (*looking, and reading*) "Apollo and the Muses".
Benjy Ta . . .
Jerome But it says so underneath!
Benjy So it does—I can't focus wi'out me specs . . . What's a Muse?
Mrs Dix (*calling*) It's a classical allegory!
Benjy Fancy . . .
Mrs Dix The nine Muses each represent something—The Muse of History, Poetry, Dancing and so forth, take your pick, ha ha . . . (*Back to her writing*)
Benjy Nine smashers, I'm impressed. (*He goes to the desk, replaces the book on a bookshelf, comes back to the stool, and sees Daisy*) Cheered up, 'ave we, since tea-time? (*With a bow*) Might I trouble your ladyship? (*He puts his hand to his ear; no answer. He shrugs, lifts up the doll and heaves it on to the sofa*)
Jerome Good shot . . .

Benjy sits on the stool. Jerome looks towards the veranda, rises abruptly, crosses to the veranda, passes Mrs Dix, and peers over the river; he is worried and nervy

Jerome This is terribly unlike her . . .
Mrs Dix Unlike her?

Jerome Lydia. Taking the dinghy across and going for a walk, there's nowhere to walk! And it's well past eleven ...

Mrs Dix She's having a good think, poor darling.

As Jerome comes back into the room ...

It'll sort itself out, mark my words. Cuckoo can be handled.

Jerome (*at the dresser, holding up a nearly empty bottle*) Has Uncle Powell been at the whisky? (*He pours two glasses*)

Benjy Tipped it into 'is bedside jug, sorry sir ...

Jerome Oh Lord ...

He sits again, opposite Benjy. They play cards; in between they take an occasional sip

Benjy Miss Lydia's not 'erself. She's passin' through a phrase.

Jerome She is indeed.

Benjy It's Cuckoo, sir, isn't it?

Jerome Dixie swears Cuckoo can be 'andled.

Benjy Cuckoo can be 'andled? Excuse me, sir, but that one's as easy to 'andle as a cartload o' monkeys. I was once a male nurse in a posh ... nursin' 'ome-to-you—no disrespeck to Miss Lydia's goofy sister, but the joint was *stuffed* wi' Cuckoos. And are they a sly bunch—*sly*! What's more, she *knows* she's sly an' what's more, she knows *I* know.

Jerome (*amused*) She does?

Benjy She does! I've caught 'er lookin' at me as if to say, "If *you* keep mum about *me*, *I'll* keep mum about *you*", gives me the willies. (*He plays a card*)

Jerome Benjy did you ever go to jail?

Benjy (*after a beat*) Not lately ... Ask me if I went to a good school.

Jerome Did you go to a good school?

Benjy (*pat*) I think I must been, 'cause it was approved, ha ...

Jerome too relishes the joke

Jerome What did you go to jail for?

Benjy Pinchin' an' punchin', punchin' an' pinchin'. Nothin' drastic.

Jerome What made you go straight?

Benjy I took sick.

Jerome What was the matter with you?

Benjy Religious mania.

Jerome Religious *mania*?

Benjy One wet night in West 'Artlepool after thirteen pints. Sally Army, Mercy Seat, the lot. Me what 'ad never 'ad a day's illness in me life!

Jerome Who converted you?

Benjy Lady friend.

Jerome Oh ... *You* got religion?

Benjy I never put me feet up but it left me very weak. She was in one o' them bonnets, I'm ashamed o' nothin'.

Jerome (*suddenly remembering*) Just a minute ... This afternoon, when you sewed that button on to my jacket—you threaded the needle!

Benjy What about it?

Jerome And you need glasses to read *that* print? (*Indicating the bookshelves*)

Benjy I'll tell you somethin', sir, 'cause I trust you. When I said I'm ashamed o' nothin', I said a lie. I can't read nor write.

Jerome (*surprised, touched*) No . . .

Benjy Ran away from the orphanage, ran away from the approved school, can't read nor write, ain't that somethin'? One posh bloke that caught me out like you jus' done, swore that "this phenomenone is unknown in this day and age"—but you'd be surprised at the number o' blokes in the same quandary as me.

Jerome "Quandary"—that's a good word!

Benjy I know, but ask me to spell it . . .

On the veranda, Mrs Dix stands up, collects her letters, puts them in her handbag and shuts the typewriter

Mrs Dix (*calling*) I don't think I'll hang on any longer . . .

Benjy (*calling*) I'll see you back, mum, to the Swan . . .

Mrs Dix (*calling*) Thank you kind sir she said, ha ha . . .

Benjy She's pure gold. If all women was like 'er—your cards—the race'd die out.

Jerome You've made a study of women, Benjy, have you?

Benjy Gettin' be'ind wi' me 'omework. Never worried me . . . much. Keep movin's my motto. Where women's concerned, two things to remember— stick to the towns, an' give a false name. Your real name confuses the issue, your cards.

Jerome What sort of false name?

Benjy Pick it up anywhere—off the election posters.

Mrs Dix comes into the room, with the typewriter and her handbag

Mrs Dix This belongs to Madam Ellis, does it not . . . (*She places it on the floor, next to the armchair, and moves to go up the the archway*)

Benjy (*to her*) Is there a Muse o' Sex?

Mrs Dix (*going*) I don't think so.

Benjy Funny . . .

Jerome Thank you, Mrs Dix, for everything——

Mrs Dix Dixie to you, you may as well get used to it!

Jerome But . . . aren't you leaving tomorrow?

Mrs Dix No no—never say die! But I won't intrude on poor Cuckoo till tomorrow afternoon, and then gently—mustn't push too fast! She hasn't exactly taken to me, but Lady Ruth Pillie didn't *speak* to me for the first three months! (*Social, a favourite story*) Just glared—then, suddenly, got up from a jigsaw puzzle, put on her brother's hat, a bowler, waltzed round the room, did a deep curtsy, and we were *pals*. I laughed to myself, the bowler and the curtsy were slightly incongruous, ha ha . . . (*She is going*)

Jerome Three months seems a long time to wait.

Mrs Dix (*turning again*) This will be quicker. She's acting, you see!

Jerome (*eagerly*) She is, isn't she——

Mrs Dix All children do, once they're the centre of attraction.

Jerome Because her mother's death was too much to take in——
Mrs Dix She has instinctively made herself believe that Lydia is her mother——
Jerome A sort of escape hatch——
Mrs Dix Exactly. (*She goes to the hatstand in the corridor, to put on her raincoat*)
Jerome She talks sense.
Benjy In this little operation, you need more than sense.
Jerome What d'you need, more than sense?
Benjy Like in the songs—'eart. This joint is full of 'eart, give the sense away nex' door, sir you owe me sevenpence, for further advice enclose stamped addressed evelope.

Mrs Dix comes back from the corridor, fastening her belt

Mrs Dix Don't fret, Mr Price ...

Benjy takes the cards to the desk, then goes up to the hatstand for his cap

  The weight will gradually move off Lydia, and on to me.
Jerome That makes sense ... (*He catches Benjy's eye*)
Mrs Dix Why don't *you* talk to her?
Jerome Me? I have tried, not much success ...
Mrs Dix I had another go at her, just trying to chat. Slippery as ever, but I did find out one thing—she likes *you*. Quite spontaneously, she suddenly said—you know the priceless way she talks—"Cuckoo got a soft spot for the man with the million thruppeny bits!"
Jerome After my money, I see. But it's something ...
Mrs Dix (*going*) So do try, it all helps!
Jerome (*half rising*) I'll come with you——
Benjy (*putting on his cap*) Desist, partner, desist ...
Mrs Dix (*to Jerome*) Tell Lydia I'll be over tomorrow afternoon. Lest *noo* acquaintance be ferrgot, ha ha ...
Jerome I'll have a bowler ready, just in case.
Mrs Dix Good-night—(*going, then turning*)—I'm sorry, what did you—(*after a beat*)—Lady *Pillie* of course, how amusing, ha ha ...

  She goes out into the kitchen; Benjy looks at Jerome and follows her

Jerome goes out to the veranda and again peers over the river. He returns, frustrated, in time to hear the noise of a chair being overturned, in Powell's room. He goes to the archway. The loud mutter of Powell's voice

Jerome (*calling, to* R) Uncle Powell!

No answer; he comes down again

  Powell comes careering into the room, in his wheelchair. He is in his nightshirt, dishevelled, and has been drinking, but looks more alive than he has earlier; he is flushed and aggressive

Powell Who the hell's been sneaking to my door?
Jerome I was worried about you——

Powell Why?

Jerome (*standing up to him*) You were talking to yourself, that's why, and swearing like a trooper——

Powell For God's sake *stop* worrying about me, too many people worry about too many people, don't do it! Got the bloody ambulance ready?

As Jerome makes for the kitchen ...

I was settled, till Moneybags walked in!

Jerome (*stung*) Moneybags? Fire away ... (*Striding to the stool, and sitting, to face Powell*) What has Moneybags done to you?

Powell (*speaking thickly, with the telescoped speech of a man drunk and angry, but articulate*) I'll tell you wha' you done to me. For sixteen years, this ugly vulgar shell of a house has sheltered this ugly vulgar shell of a body—but more'n that. It's been a monastery, for my *mind*. Every day for sixteen years, with a rhythm as regular as light and dark, I used to read a book. Every day, while my body stayed put, my mind was ... a bird. Every inch of this place meant—adventure. Three summers ago, I sat next to a grubby lilac bush, wi' dictionary I was reading Virgil, *arma virumque cano* ... Punts were golden barges, those vile gramophones carried music of heavenly harps, the sparrows were doves, wallflowers smelt of ambrosia, I was *rich*, Mr Price and Son, rich and at peace. (*Wheeling himself, abruptly*) Good-night——

Jerome No you don't——(*He swings the wheelchair round*)

Powell (*savagely*) What the hell——

Jerome And what's Moneybags done to you?

Powell Ruined it! Uncle's to be slung into a net, is he, wi' the other luggage, is he, an' bundled into a cabin. I'd have you know, sir, that within these four walls I've been on more pleasure-cruises than your father could ever afford, and you've ruined it. (*In a shout*) Ruined ... (*Taking Jerome's arm, suddenly piteous and contrite*) I insulted you an' called you Moneybags, I meant no harm ... (*Gulping, maudlin*)

Jerome Uncle Powell, you're not being honest, are you?

Powell (*glaring at him*) Me, not honest?

Jerome It's not Moneybags who's done this to you. It's Mam, isn't it?

Powell (*indignant, bluffing*) No! (*Looking at him*) Yes ... (*More sober*) It never occurred to me that she ... might go first. These things happen to other people, that's why we buy the papers ... (*The words blurred and jumbled*) I can't sleep at night. When I was ten years old my dog was run over, I buried him in a field. I woke up that night and heard the wind howling—howling over my lost darling, cold 'n' lonely in the ground ... (*Weeping, maudlin*) What's happened to me—my mind had wings, where are they? My mind is pinned to the ground like my potato of a body—(*a cry of rage*)—I can't move my mind!

The bedroom door opens and Cuckoo wanders in. She is in her dressing-gown over a nightdress, and barefoot

Cuckoo (*worried*) Mam back? Where's Mam ...

Powell (*to Jerome angrily*) But why am I inflicting this on you ... ?

Cuckoo (*timidly*) Uncle Powell s-scolding?
Jerome Scolding himself.
Cuckoo Is he being naughty?
Powell Behaving like a child, more like a child than she is. (*Wheeling himself towards the archway, and almost running into Cuckoo*) Out of my way!

She shrinks from him, with a cry

He wheels himself to his room

Jerome and Cuckoo are alone. He sits in the armchair, dejected. She wanders down and sits on the stool. He takes in that she is there, and sits carefully up, facing her

Jerome Cuckoo ... somebody told me that you like me.
Cuckoo (*swiftly, unexpectedly*) Oh *yes*! You walk so quick, and your shoes and your tie-pin and you talk like the warning to all shipping a depression on the Fairy Islands! (*Her attitude to him is not crafty, as with Mrs Dix: friendly and candid*)
Jerome Lydia and I are going to get married.

She looks up at him; her smiles has faded. The guard is up again

Cuckoo L-Lydia?
Jerome Lydia and I are going to get married.
Cuckoo C-Cuckoo got a pain.
Jerome You heard what I said——
Cuckoo (*suddenly, happily*) Mam!

She rises and lumbers over to greet ...

Lydia as she appears from the garden and into the room. Lydia looks tired and preoccupied: wearing a jacket, a light scarf over her head

Lydia (*embracing her, mechanically*) Darling—have you been all right ...
Cuckoo Cuckoo all right, now Mam back ...
Jerome I was having a little chat with Cuckoo.
Lydia Oh yes ...
Jerome More than I've been able to have with you.
Lydia I wanted to walk.

Cuckoo goes to the sofa, takes Daisy up, and settles down as if to sleep. Lydia takes off her jacket

Jerome Did you come to a decision?

Lydia shakes her head, helplessly

Lydia Was your "little chat" helpful? (*She goes up to the hatstand to hang up her jacket*)
Jerome Hardly.
Cuckoo (*her eyes still closed*) Silly-Billy ...
Jerome Silly-Billy, me?
Cuckoo T-talking about getting married to Lydia.

Lydia Was he? (*Carefully*) Why would it be silly?

Cuckoo Because Lydia's gone away.

Lydia For good?

Cuckoo For good. (*Sitting up, suddenly*) So Mam ... why doesn't he marry *you*? (*Her head against Lydia's skirt*)

Lydia and Jerome look at each other. He rises, and goes up to Cuckoo. He and Lydia are standing on either side of her

Jerome Cuckoo ... that's a splendid idea! Do you think ... she'll have me?

Cuckoo Why don't you ask her?

Jerome (*carefully, to Lydia*) Will you marry me?

Lydia (*after a pause, uncertainly*) Yes ... I will.

Cuckoo (*clapping her hands*) Oh, lovely!

Jerome You like the idea?

Cuckoo Oh yes, because Mam can share in the thruppenny bits! The least she deserves after a hard life working the bone off her fingers! Think of when the gold band is slipped on and the little word is whispered *I will* look out for next instalment ... (*Singing*) "The bells are ringin', For me an' my gal ..." Daisy never been to a wedding, have you ducky-wucky? (*To Jerome*) What will the bride wear?

Jerome (*warming to it*) White, yards and yards——

Lydia (*likewise*) And what colour would Cuckoo like?

Cuckoo B-baby blue! There was a wedding in "Funny Ole London" on the wireless ... (*Joining their hands*) "To have and to ... hold" ...

Lydia Then the wedding breakfast——

Cuckoo (*eyes closed, rapt*) B-baby blue ... And after breakfast?

Lydia The bride goes up to change——

Cuckoo And then she f-floats down the stairs——

Jerome Steps into a car, an old boot on the back, look out for next instalment!

Cuckoo (*clapping her hands*) Lovely! And then where do we go?

Jerome We?

Her eyes tell them that she is perfectly sincere; slowly, their hands fall apart

Cuckoo A l-lady and gentleman on the wireless went for *their* honeymoon to a place called It-Italy, and stayed with an old lady named Florence! Will *we*?

She shuts her eyes, with a happy sigh. Jerome and Lydia look at each other; Jerome walks down, desperate

Jerome Something'll happen—something *must*.

Lydia (*to Cuckoo*) Bed darling.

Cuckoo Beddibyes?

Lydia Beddibyes ...

She helps Cuckoo up with the doll, puts her arms round her and leads her to the bedroom door

Cuckoo goes in

(*At the door, calling*) One-two-three—into bed! There ... (*Closing the door and coming back to Jerome*) Let her sleep, poor unhappy baby.

Jerome Let her sleep, while you have a look on your face I've never seen before. Bitterness.

Lydia (*sitting back in the armchair*) I thought I was looking sensible.

Jerome I can be sensible too. I know what you're thinking—"I have a duty, to my helpless sister——"

Lydia Don't make it harder for me——

Jerome By facing the facts?

Lydia I can't think any more. What am I to do? Tell me ...

Jerome I will, and it won't take long. She's determined to keep you to herself. But we can get determined too. She's playing us up.

Lydia I know, but it's her terrible ... desolation which she can't express— that's what's doing it——

Jerome Lydia, listen to me! (*Sitting on the arm of the chair*) At this minute, your life is in your own hands, you're holding it there—(*cupping his fingers*)—and a more promising plant there never was. And what are you proposing to do? To turn that plant away from the sun, and let it wither. You owe it to yourself—*please* believe me—and to her! To make a clean break, *now*—to grab her by the arm and jolt her into reality. We're going to leave her.

Lydia Leave her?

Jerome With Mrs Dix.

Lydia She turned against Mrs Dix——

Jerome At first she did—but she suspected *me*, at first! Mrs Dix will be firm without ever being unkind, you *must* see that——

Lydia I do, everything you say is right——

Jerome Let's sleep on it, and in the morning we'll think it over and make a solid plan. Will you leave it to me?

The door of Madam's room opens quietly and she appears in the archway

Lydia (*rising*) All right, we'll think it over.

Madam, relieved to see them still up, steps forward. Lydia crosses to the bedroom. In Powell's bedroom, loud muttering

Powell (*off*) What the hell—(*hiccuping*)—what the hell's the point of it all ...

Jerome There goes Uncle Powell, he's been on the rampage once already.

Lydia Oh no——

Madam (*listening*) My brother is talking to himself. And hiccuping.

Jerome Did he wake you up?

Madam I *was* awake. (*She comes down. She looks very different from when last seen; she wears no make-up, is in a loose pale dressing-gown, and her hair is disarranged. For the first time, we see her subdued, nervy even, upset*) I ... (*Putting her hand to her face, and swaying a little*)

Jerome When in doubt, brandy ... (*He goes to the dresser and pours a brandy*)

Madam Oh dear, is it wise, do you think ... It's terribly quiet on my side, did you know ... (*Taking the glass from Jerome*) And I miss the moon, makes such a difference ... (*Drinking*) Lovely and warm *evviva il vino*, but brandy isn't *vino*, is it, or is it ... Thank God you're still up, this is a bad time of night, these days ...

Jerome I'm sorry you're feeling low——

Madam I don't often, Liddy, do I? (*To Jerome*) But this ... having happened ... It's upset me more than I thought it ever could ... It's when the crying stops, that the real thing starts. "My aching heart"—I've sung that from here to the Equator and back, I never thought of it as being true. These last weeks I've been planning and spending—but in the night, I've felt my heart ... aching ... literally, I never realized it could do that ... (*Her hand to her breast, she is on the point of breaking down*)

Jerome sits her in the armchair

Lydia (*sitting on the stool*) It's ... grief, my darling, and it'll get better——

Madam More than grief. Regret. Conscience.

Lydia Conscience?

Madam I don't think I've ever said that aloud before! ... I was your age, on top of the world. We'd been married three years.

Lydia Married?

Madam Only Mam knew.

Lydia Who was he?

Madam Mmm? A Welsh boy. (*The words alternately trickling and pouring out, the tone impersonal*) Rudolph in *Bohême*, inclined to sing flat, not a thought in his head, a straw in the wind. Poor boy, I was the wind ... He woke up one morning in the English chapel in Saltzburg.

Lydia Those three years—were they happy?

Madam He irritated me, but I was fond of him. He *loved* me. Loved me as Mam loved Cuckoo.

Lydia What was he like?

Madam Just a nice Welsh boy with a lot of love and a lot of poor health. We were singing in Paris ... (*The next words are the ones she finds hardest to bring out*) The doctor told me he was ... incurable, and he would have to be nursed with devotion. That's the word he used, *dévotion* ...

Jerome And what happened? (*Sitting, on the right arm of her chair*)

Madam I was taken up—madly, irrevocably—with a painter, Jacques—Jules—oh God, I can't remember his name ... (*Recovering*) I went to the hospital, told ... my husband. He said he understood, I kissed him goodbye. A prima-donna kiss, on the brow, I remember thinking, how noble I am ... I turned at the door. Great feverish brown eyes. His arm was flung out, a patch of sweat on the hospital shirt, that bit is *not* in my Life Story ... Walking down the stairs, I looked out, *les toits de Paris*, every time I hear that tune ... Above the roofs, in the sky, I saw his face. I'm seeing it now. I've always run away from death. But when your sister ... goes, it's a tug at your elbow. What's the aria from some damn opera—*Let us depart in glory*, pom pom ... Liddy, your mother departed in glory, because she had given ... devotion. I have nothing to depart in—

no glory, nothing. (*She finishes her brandy and rises, abruptly breaking the mood*) He only lived a year, so I wouldn't have had to wait long. And it would have been good to look back on, at a moment like this. (*Handing her glass to Lydia*) Having said all that, in the morning I shan't remember a thing.

Lydia Conscience ...

Madam Not your concern, *cara*, you've got your lovely future——

Lydia It *is* my concern.

Madam But how?

Jerome Cuckoo. (*Sitting in the armchair*)

Madam Cuckoo? What a silly-sounding word ... But this Mrs Dix is going to take charge of her, it's simple!

Lydia (*rising briskly*) It isn't simple at all, bed everybody ... (*Crossing to the desk, putting down Madam's glass and turning off a lamp*) Jerome, see you in the morning——

Madam She's absurd but even I can tell she's efficient, and you can't expect Cuckoo to take to her like *that* ...

Jerome That's what *I* said ...

Lydia She depends on me, and always will ...

Jerome And Lydia feels that it calls for a change of plan.

Madam A change of plan, what do you mean?

Jerome No wedding.

Madam (*appalled*) No ... wedding? But—my flat?

Lydia And the new dresses ...

Madam *No wedding*! Lydia, stuff and nonsense!

Benjy enters from the kitchen, wearing his cap

Mrs Dix is the solution, of course it'll work——

As she goes up to the archway, a loud crash in Powell's room, then the smashing of glass. Jerome rises

Benjy 'Ello, 'ello, 'ello ...

Powell (*off*) Matches—gimme *matches* ...

Benjy 'E's off again ...

Jerome All hands on deck ...

Madam Not these hands. I'm an escapist—*Dio mio*, this house is turning into the Villa Malcontenta, *ciao*!

She hurries into her room and bangs the door shut

Lydia What is he up to—I'll go in——

Powell comes racing on from his room; his hair is wild, and he is a couple of stages more drunk than before

Powell (*hoarse and breathless*) Matches——

Benjy Steady partner, what can we do for *you*——

From now to the curtain, the action goes very quickly

Powell (*panting*) Matches? What for?

Cuckoo stumbles in from the bedroom, barefoot, in her nightdress. She is frightened—terrified

Benjy (*to her*) 'Ello 'ello, ever 'eard o' bedtime, naughty girl ...

Cuckoo runs across to Lydia and clings to her

Powell Set fire to all those bloody books in there, an' go for a walk! (*His voice rising to a childish shout*) A *walk*!
Lydia (*to Cuckoo*) It's all right, my love——
Jerome (*in a shout*) Uncle Powell, *go to bed*!
Benjy Leave 'im to me sir, Strait-jacket Jack, that's me——
Powell (*in a snarl, overturning the small table*) MATCHES! Walk—stride the countryside, seven-league boots, set the bloody place on fire—(*driving his chair round*)—matches—desk——
Benjy Don't be ridiculous Nicholas. Or I'll 'ave to start callin' you names——
Powell I'll call myself a name—*potato*! Walk walk walk—desk—(*In a shout*)—MATCHES!
Benjy (*spinning the chair round, in a sergeant-major bawl*) QUI-ET!

This has its effect; Powell sits panting, glaring at Benjy. From the river, growing louder, feverish jazz music

You cruel selfish thing, wakin' up Nest O' Robinsons, shh ... Come on Spud ... (*Starting to wheel the chair up to the archway*)
Powell *NO!*

He gives a sudden twist to his chair; Benjy makes to pull him round again, but this time Powell wins; at the desk, he clutches it in both hands, just as Benjy pulls the chair, right from under him. As Powell topples to the floor, Jerome rushes to him, hiding the body from the audience; he and Benjy kneel. Lydia is holding Cuckoo's head, so that she cannot see

Benjy Oh my gawd ... Just look at you, you bad lad!
Lydia What is it?
Benjy Come out wi'out 'is legs.
Lydia No!
Powell (*muttering, viciously*) Potato——
Benjy Sorry miss. (*To Powell*) You careless thing——
Cuckoo Without his l-legs?
Lydia It's all right, darling——
Benjy Don't worry ducks, we'll cover 'im up, poor chap ... (*To Powell*) Come on chum, beddybies——
Powell (*muttering*) Seven league boots—ho ho ho—boots boots boots ... (*His voice trailing off into silence*)
Jerome Passed out——
Benjy Good thing too——
Cuckoo Is he d-dead?
Lydia (*holding her*) It's *all right* ...
Benjy It's a shame though, ain't it, eh? Jus' like one o' them beat-up statues from the olden days——

Jerome Let's get him into the chair——

Lydia runs across, and holds the chair from behind. Cuckoo turns round, takes a step, and peers at Powell's overturned body

Benjy For short weight, 'e's a 'andfull! (*As he and Jerome hold Powell, each by one arm*) One two...
Cuckoo (*fascinated, horrified*) It's true ... He hasn't got ... (*Turning*)
Jerome *Three!*

The two heave Powell into the wheelchair, just as Lydia runs back to Cuckoo and holds her

Cuckoo (*in shock*) It's true ...
Benjy Time for shut-eye, me ole ruffian ...

   Jerome takes the wheelchair and wheels it smartly to the archway and to R

   I told 'im 'e should never ha' gone for that walk on that French beach. (*Calling*) Wait for me!

   Benjy follows Jerome off

Cuckoo, pressed to Lydia, sobs quietly, but uncontrollably, as the Lights fade, the music swells, and the CURTAIN *falls. It rises again, immediately, on ...*

<h2 style="text-align:center">SCENE 2</h2>

As the CURTAIN *rises, the music melts imperceptibly into a sad tune which comes from the wireless set on the desk*

The next morning; sunlight. The bedroom door is closed. On the small table, a stocking, with needle and thread

Cuckoo sits huddled in the desk-chair, deep in sorrowful thought; she is again barefoot under her dressing-gown. Her handbag is beside her

Benjy comes in from the kitchen, whistling; he is back in his green-baize apron, and carries a watering-can. Passing Cuckoo, he notices her depression

Benjy Come on, snap out of it!

She does not react. He shrugs, goes to the dresser and waters the plant. Cuckoo switches off the wireless and turns to go to the bedroom

   (*Watering*) What you goin' to do today, ducks? Feed the swans? Give Daisy 'er dinner? Read the *Radio Times*? Oh, sorry, you can't read, I forgot ...

Cuckoo halts; her back is to Benjy, but it seems almost to bristle with offence. She wheels slowly round, looks at the bookshelves, comes down, takes up a book, opens it, and walks slowly across, as if reading. She bumps slightly into the sofa. Benjy comes down to go into the kitchen, then sees the book, and stands watching her. She sits sedately in the armchair, her eyes still on the printed page

I never seed you wi' a book before.
Cuckoo Cuckoo not been reading for donkey's years. (*Not looking up*)

Benjy stares at her, starts to go, then looks back

Benjy Enjoyin' it?
Cuckoo Yes thank you, silly Lady Pillie ...

Benjy puts down the watering-can, selects a coin from a pocket, and crosses to the stool

Benjy See this 'and? (*Holding it out, closed*)
Cuckoo (*looking up*) Yes?
Benjy What 'ave I got in my fist?
Cuckoo A thruppenny bit.
Benjy You're abso-bally-lutely right! An' you can 'ave it in *your* fist ... (*sitting on the stool*) ... if you describe me the book you're readin'. (*As she looks at him*) Now.
Cuckoo It's g-green, with wee black things all over the place. (*Holding out her hand*)
Benjy Oh no you don't ... (*Taking another coin, as she goes back to her book*) I'll jump the ante to *two* thruppenny bits——

She looks up; he is holding out a sixpence

—if you read out ... (*pointing to a paragraph*) ... them words.
Cuckoo (*after a pause, looking down at her book*) "When the k-king entered the forest in s-search of the princess, d-dragons of every shape and s-size." (*Holding out her hand*)
Benjy (*staring*) Thank you. (*Handing her the sixpence*)
Cuckoo (*putting it away in her bag*) Do you like being read to?
Benjy (*thoughtful*) Yes ...

She places her open book on his knee; he looks down at it

Cuckoo Will *you* read to *me*?

Benjy looks at her, then down at the book

Benjy I can't focus wi'out me specs. (*Handing her back the book*)
Cuckoo Thank you.

She puts the book down, still open at the page, face downwards, rises, and walks sedately to the bedroom

Benjy looks after her, then down at the book. He shakes his head, rises and goes towards the kitchen

Jerome enters from the kitchen, wearing a panama

Lydia (*calling, off, in the bedroom*) Are you all right. . . ?
Jerome Morning, Benjy . . . (*Crossing him, then putting a weary hand to his eyes*)
Benjy Mornin' sir . . . Bad night?
Jerome I was worried about Uncle Powell. (*He sits in the armchair*)
Benjy Don't you fret yerself sir, I took 'im in 'is tea at seven as per usual, 'e was sittin' up, very thoughtful like, not a peep out of 'im, good as new.
Jerome No! . . . That's a relief.
Benjy An' when I fixed 'is legs, 'e was a babe in these tender 'an's. Know what I am, under the concrete? Womanish. I am!

He goes into the kitchen

Jerome takes off his hat

Lydia comes in from the bedroom, closing the door; she ties on an apron. She is dressed for the day; under some strain, she is determinedly neat and business-like. They face each other, then their emotion makes them turn quickly away

Lydia Good-morning Jerome, you're early, aren't you tired——
Jerome I have to go and cancel the furniture-van for tomorrow.
Lydia Of course . . .
Jerome Aren't *you* tired?
Lydia (*with an effort*) I feel surprisingly fresh. (*She starts to replace books on the bookshelves*)
Jerome How is she?
Lydia Well . . . (*Concerned*) Most mornings she wakes up with the birds, chattering away. This morning no, when I woke I thought she was asleep. Then I saw her eyes were wide open.
Jerome Is she ill?
Lydia No, no temperature . . .
Jerome Mind you, last night must have done something terrible to her.
Lydia You mean Uncle Powell . . .
Jerome Yes . . .
Lydia Poor lamb . . .
Jerome Who's the poor lamb, him or her?
Lydia (*catching his irony*) Either.
Jerome And Madam?
Lydia (*brightening*) On the warpath!
Jerome Good for her . . .
Lydia Singing scales, back in a world of her own. (*Crossing, to the veranda*) She's done what she said she would—pushed the whole thing out of her mind. (*Craning*) Look at her, sitting back in the dinghy as if it were a gondola.
Jerome You slept, did you?
Lydia In the end, yes. (*Leaning against the corner of the veranda door*) I kept hearing Madam's voice. Not singing scales but what she told us last night, sitting there. I never thought I'd get the right advice from that quarter.
Jerome The right advice?
Lydia Last night, walking those back streets past the little houses, I thought

of the people inside. I realized something about myself which—before these last weeks, if somebody'd said it—I'd have taken for a joke. I realized that I've led a sheltered life.

Jerome Sheltered? You?

Lydia Sheltered from what I'm having to face now. (*Almost to herself*) Those little houses—and big houses, everywhere—are full of people who've had to give up . . . something important. Single women with a bed-ridden mother, husbands loyal to a wife they don't love any more, relatives saddled with an unwanted baby—those blank faces opposite me in the train every day . . . When you belong in a family, sooner or later . . . (*walking from the veranda*) . . . you have to take on . . . responsibility. Conscience . . . Mam had her responsibility, and tied herself for life. How can I shirk *my* responsibility . . . (*she is near breaking down*) . . . and look her in the face?

From a punt on the river, a waltz

Jerome Water-music. Remember?

Lydia The taste of the champagne.

As she crosses him, he takes her into his arms. They almost kiss, but she avoids it. She presses her head against him, then makes herself stand away from him. She starts for the bedroom

Jerome Your mother . . .

As she turns to him . . .

For a mild little woman who was always doing housework, she has certainly left her mark.

Lydia smiles, sadly, opens the bedroom door and looks in

Lydia Why are you still lying down—now get up, love and *dress*—I'm mending your stockings so put the other pair on . . . What? . . . You want what, I can't hear you, what is it . . .

She disappears into the bedroom

Jerome looks after her, and sits dejectedly back in the armchair

Lydia hurries back from the bedroom and takes up the telephone, consulting a list of numbers

Lydia (*into the telephone*) Emberbrook nine-nine-two-four. . . . Swan Hotel? . . . Room twenty-four, Mrs Dix.

Jerome Mrs Dix?

Lydia (*after a pause, into the telephone*) Hello, you slept well? . . . Good—could you come over as soon as you can, she wants to see you. . . . Cuckoo! . . . I don't know, she just kept whispering "I want to see Doctor Dix, I want to see Doctor Dix." . . . I agree, it *is* a good sign—can you come over, now? . . . Good. . . . (*Hanging up, and turning to Jerome*) *Doctor* Dix—why Doctor?

Jerome That must be me—after the lady left yesterday afternoon, I tried to do a little spadework with Cuckoo, by telling her that Dixie can help people with something wrong with them, and she must have got it into her head that she's a real doctor, like your father was.

Lydia The poor child obviously isn't well ... (*coming down to the stool, sitting, and taking up Cuckoo's stocking, to finish mending a hole in it*)

Jerome Could she be *taking* to her?

Lydia To dear old Dixie? Not on your life. She's worried about herself, nothing new ...

Madam hurries in from the garden, holding an empty cup of coffee; she is her old buoyant self, flowing with optimism (and make-up). She hands Jerome her cup

Madam (*to Lydia, excited*) Carissima, I have the most *wonderful* idea!

Lydia What?

Madam That Cuckoo should spend half of every year with *me*!

With an ironical shake of the head, Jerome goes out on to the veranda and sits, in disconsolate thought

Liddy, what do you say?

Lydia (*mending*) It wouldn't work.

Madam *Lydia*! But I make her laugh—when I trill away and play the fool, she *rolls* about!

Lydia You can't be trilling from morning till night while she's rolling, you'd both be worn out.

Madam (*giggling*) Beast ... (*On top again, taking a step towards the veranda inhaling*) What a Riviera morning, *molto allegro*, sleep well?

Lydia (*pointedly*) Did you?

Madam Never lifted my head from the pillow ... Shall I tell you what I've been planning, with Jerome's help and a guarantee of his money back? A lecture tour on Opera right through the States! (*Hurrying to the desk*) I shall write to my old agent, this minute——

Lydia (*mending*) Jerome's going up to London to tell his father we can't get married.

Madam Rubbish. (*Starting to scribble*) Something tells me that Papa will make him see sense. I absolutely *refuse* to throw in the sponge!

Lydia Madam Ellis is talking like a punch-drunk old boxer.

Madam Madam Ellis *is* an old boxer. *Cara*, if Mrs Dix doesn't work somebody else will come along!

Lydia (*wearily*) Cuckoo will never take to anybody new—last night, did you *dream* that you came sleepwalking in here? And *talked* in your sleep?

Madam Humanity is at its lowest ebb in the small hours. *Not* the time for making merry—imagine waking up at two a.m., listening to the owls and going into the Jewel Song, can't be done!

The telephone rings

Lydia (*rising and going to answer it*) Madam dear, we're not singing the Jewel Song to an audience of owls, we're coping with my sister—(*Into the telephone*) Yes?

Madam Nothing to do with it——

Lydia (*to her*) It's another Madam, Madam Yvonne.

Madam (*excited*) My fitting! My dear, the most resplendent number, give it to me——

Lydia (*into the telephone, gentle but firm*) I'm terribly sorry, but I'm afraid Madam Ellis has had to change her plans——

Madam What?

Lydia She has to cancel the dress, it's too bad, goodbye ... (*Replacing the receiver*) It had to be done. (*Going back to the stool*)

Madam (*rising, ablaze with operatic indignation*) Lydia Roberts, you slip of a girl, how *dare* you! You're behaving like a *man*! Plans changed indeed ... (*She turns to see...*)

Cuckoo enters from the bedroom, dressed. Cuckoo, looking at nobody, drifts to the sofa, sad, preoccupied

Madam smiles confidently at Lydia, and takes a step towards Cuckoo

(*Playful, winning*) Cuck-*oo*!

No response. Madam breaks into song

"I am the Maid of Japan, who was betrayed by a Man!"

No response; Cuckoo's face is expressionless as she sits on the sofa

Lydia Bang goes the flat in St John's Wood.

Madam It has central heating, and parquet, and *panelling*—Liddy, *where* am I going to live?

Lydia As you were, I'm afraid—here. (*She finishes her mending*)

Madam *Here*? Stuff and double nonsense! (*Bouncing right up again*) Do you know what I'm going to do, with my own hands? (*Sitting back at the desk, to continue her letter*) I'm going to pack my case, *exactly* as if I were going back to the Savoy to sign the lease of my flat, *voilà*! Something will happen, I feel it in my bones, *avanti*!

A knock at the kitchen door, and Mrs Dix bustles in. She wears a flowered hat: roses

Lydia (*rising*) Ah—good-morning Mrs Dix——

Jerome on the veranda, sees Mrs Dix, rises, and comes into the room

Mrs Dix (*in the highest of spirits*) Dixie to you, top o' the morning to all and sundry! (*To Madam*) Or, Madam Ellis, should I say "top-*note* o' the morning", ha ha ...

Madam closes her eyes, takes up her letter and pen, rises, sweeps up to her room, banging the door behind her

Mrs Dix, sublimely unaware, is taking off her gloves

So my little friend has asked for me! A ray of light, what did I tell you? It's exciting, I *shot* over——

Cuckoo has not moved; she sits downcast

Lydia Would you like some tea?

Mrs Dix Just a wee pot, very weak, that would be scrumptious, you are a poppet, nothing to nibble—she wants to tell me her weeny aches and pains, oddies are often a tidge hypochondriac, doncher know!

Lydia goes towards the kitchen. Jerome crosses to her

Jerome May I offer my assistance in making the tea?

Lydia Thank you——

Jerome It might make me feel useful. Not just hanging around.

Lydia (*smiling, sadly*) I know how you feel . . .

She goes into the kitchen, followed by Jerome, who closes the door

Cuckoo and Mrs Dix are alone

Mrs Dix (*crossing, and sitting in the armchair*) Well dear, here we are again!

Cuckoo (*looking at her coldly*) Dixie g-got a different hat.

Mrs Dix Full marks for noticing! I got it in a sale, it's the first time on! Do you like it?

Cuckoo (*politely*) No.

Mrs Dix (*undeterred*) Roses, aren't they sweet? Don't you like flowers?

Cuckoo Only in the garden, or in a pot. Cuckoo got a rose-bush.

Mrs Dix Your dear little patch of garden, of course . . .

Cuckoo It is important to water flowers. F-flowers get thirsty.

Mrs Dix Ah—Mam told you that, I bet! Now tell me, *how* are you feeling——

Cuckoo (*an instinctive interruption, to evade the issue*) An' wot 'ave you been adoin' of? (*Winnie Whitechapel*)

Mrs Dix (*humouring*) Since I was here last night? I was taken over the river to that nice Swan Hotel by the dear little ferry——

Cuckoo Did you f-fall in?

Mrs Dix (*archly*) Were you hoping I would?

Cuckoo Once a lady fell in with a fur coat and a doggie and an umbrella but I was in bed with a c-cold.

Mrs Dix Did she get wet, in the water?

Cuckoo No.

Mrs Dix Are you *sure*, dear? How did she keep dry?

Cuckoo She put the umbrella up.

Mrs Dix (*tolerantly*) That can't be *quite* true.

Cuckoo (*wearily*) The lady swam home with the doggies in her m-mouth.

Mrs Dix You sent for me, Cuckoo, remember——

Cuckoo (*quickly, evading again*) And what did you do then?

Mrs Dix Then I . . . Ah . . . (*A sigh of frustration*) Then I ventured into the hotel dining-room in search of a cup of Ovaltine——

Cuckoo It was the Cricketers' Ball, wasn't it? A lot of people dancing together?

Mrs Dix (*tersely*) No dear, it was nearly midnight, just two waitresses.

Cuckoo D-dancing together?

Mrs Dix *No* dear . . . (*Firmly*) Now what does the patient want to ask Doctor Dix?

Cuckoo hesitates, then rises, wanders down, and sits on the sofa. She is no longer acting. Mrs Dix takes her notepad from her bag

Did you sleep well?

A pause. Cuckoo's face clouds over; she is visibly distressed by what she is thinking of

Cuckoo No.
Mrs Dix (*professionally*) *Why* didn't you?
Cuckoo (*after a pause*) S-something on Cuckoo's m-mind.
Mrs Dix Is it Daisy? Your doll?
Cuckoo (*indifferent*) Daisy can look after herself.
Mrs Dix *Can* she? But you loved her——
Cuckoo Cuckoo dropped her out of the kitchen window. By the d-dustbin.
Mrs Dix (*making a note*) "Discards doll" ... (*To herself, professional*) Very interesting, bravo ... Then who is it you're worried about?

Cuckoo seems about to tell, but her distress makes her panic, and evade the issue again

Cuckoo (*desperately, her eyes shut*) The old c-cat in Hickidoola, one foot in the grave——
Mrs Dix Answer me, please—is it your sister Lydia? No, of course, Lydia's gone away ... I mean, is it ... Mam?
Cuckoo (*matter-of-fact*) No, Lydia's here. Mam's dead.
Mrs Dix (*after a pause, carefully*) Dead?
Cuckoo (*again matter-of-fact*) Mam's in Heaven.
Mrs Dix (*gently*) Of course she is, bless her ... *Is* it Lydia?
Cuckoo No.
Mrs Dix Madam? No, can't be ... But there's nobody left!
Cuckoo (*the truth, at last*) Yes there is.
Mrs Dix Who?
Cuckoo The d-damaged person.
Mrs Dix (*puzzled*) You mean ... you?
Cuckoo Cuckoo? No, Cuckoo's got no damage, not really. Cuckoo's just special, poor thing. (*Her attitude, from now on, is that of a normal mother, deeply distressed*) All the years Cuckoo and him been here together ... they never said!
Mrs Dix (*at a loss*) What?
Cuckoo He hasn't ... He hasn't g-got any legs.
Mrs Dix You mean—your Uncle Powell?
Cuckoo *He*'s got the damage.

Gradually, agonizedly, she dissolves into tears. Mrs Dix rises, very concerned, but still professional

Mrs Dix But I was told—you didn't like him?
Cuckoo Because they said he l-*liked* sitting in a chair because he was a Lazy-Bones! Why didn't they t-tell the truth?
Mrs Dix Because it would frighten you——

Cuckoo You're a doctor, doctors can do *anything*, these days, Mam said. Can you ... get him n-new legs?

Mrs Dix No dear. You see, he's got dummy ones—for the look of the thing, you see. He can't walk with them——

Cuckoo (*frantic, trying not to break down, but not succeeding*) Did it hurt? Did he cry? Who held his hand when he saw the knife?

Mrs Dix (*thinking she is of help*) No dear, there wasn't a knife, it was in the war. His legs were blown away, they couldn't be found anywhere!

Cuckoo (*appalled*) No ...

Mrs Dix He was in great pain, of course, but don't let that worry you now——

Cuckoo When Cuckoo had two stitches, Mam was s-singing to make it better. Who was sitting by *him*, to make it better?

Mrs Dix (*in a comforting voice*) A very nice nurse with a mask on.

Cuckoo (*appalled again*) No ...

Mrs Dix I know—it was Mam!

Cuckoo But Mam's dead, he hasn't got *anybody*! Last night, the two of them got him into his ch-chair and put him to bye-byes—but if they hadn't, he'd have been like the p-puppy in the story when he got caught in the trap and was dragging along crying, not a living soul to help ... And silly Lady Pillie could jump two feet ... (*Rising, walking a step up, and looking towards the archway*) There he is in there, sitting on his bed with a r-rug over his poor dummy legs, somebody should help him——

Mrs Dix (*brisk, well-meant as always*) He's used to it, dear, it was all a long time ago—and nothing to do with you!

Cuckoo turns and looks her in the face

Cuckoo (*in a measured, deadly voice*) Nothing ... to do ... with me?

Mrs Dix Nothing!

Cuckoo (*still looking at her, in the same voice*) Dixie ... doesn't understand ... *anything*.

Between the two of them, the shutter is down for good

> *Lydia comes in from the kitchen, carrying a small tray of tea; she is followed by Jerome, with a jug of milk*

Mrs Dix (*to Cuckoo*) Oh, you mustn't think that ...

Lydia Well?

Mrs Dix Cuckoo and I have just had a grand pow-wow!

Jerome (*eagerly*) You have?

Mrs Dix She's talked to me more in the last five minutes, than she has to anybody for years!

Lydia What?

Jerome She's talked to *you*?

Lydia What about?

Cuckoo has not moved; she continues to look at Mrs Dix, with an ominous lack of expression

Mrs Dix Dolls and things, and cabbages and kings!

Benjy enters from the kitchen, carrying a small carpet-sweeper, and goes towards the archway

It's a matter of time what buddies Dixie and Cuckoo are going to be!

Benjy stops and stares, incredulous

Lydia What splendid news——
Cuckoo (*suddenly*) Can Cuckoo give Dixie her tea?
Lydia (*pleased*) Of course you can! (*Taking up the teapot, in its tea-cosy*)
Benjy 'As she ever done this before? (*He puts down the carpet-sweeper*)
Lydia (*handing the teapot to Cuckoo*) Never, only with Mam! (*She sits in the armchair, to watch*)
Jerome I can't believe it——

As Cuckoo advances slowly, carefully, with the teapot

Mrs Dix (*social, happy*) It's a matter of manipulating the mind, like massage—breaking down the hard core, inspiring affection——

Slowly, impersonally, like a mutinous baby overturning a bowl of milk, she pours tea, from a height, steadily on to Mrs Dix's hat, circling the teapot round as if watering. From Mrs Dix, a sharp scream; everybody, except Cuckoo, talks at once; pandemonium. Cuckoo remains unperturbed. Jerome seizes the teapot, as Cuckoo sits in the armchair

(*Pulling off the hat and shaking it wildly*) Oh—what—my hat—my roses——

Jerome takes the hat from her

—wet through——

As Jerome pilots her into the kitchen, a completely demoralized expert on psychology . . .

—but what happened—my new hat—my hair . . .

Jerome and Mrs Dix exit to the kitchen

Lydia (*frantic*) Cuckoo, what on earth——
Benjy 'Ot tea, she could 'a scalded to death——
Lydia Get her to the tap—Cuckoo, how *could* you—her hat, you've *drenched* it!
Cuckoo It is imp-important to water flowers.

Benjy starts to laugh; Lydia tries to control her amusement, but has to laugh too

Jerome returns from the kitchen, holding the drenched hat. He is sober-faced, till he sees their faces

All three are overwhelmed in infectious laughter

Lydia (*sobering*) How is she?

Jerome Right off her perch, I'm afraid—walked straight out.
Lydia How awful—I must try and catch her ...

She runs out into the kitchen

Benjy Them lovely rose-leaves, jus' look at 'em!
Jerome They're tea-leaves now ... Cuckoo, what on earth possessed you?
Cuckoo It is important to water flowers.

Benjy takes up the tray and goes towards the kitchen

Jerome But you can't water flowers with hot tea!
Benjy The artificial ones you can water wi' anything.

He goes into the kitchen

Jerome shakes the hat, goes out on to the veranda, and hangs it up to dry

Powell emerges smartly from his room, in his chair, a desk-drawer in his lap, on his tray. He is neat and tidy

Powell (*in the archway, his head averted, blurting dutifully*) I wish to apologize to you all ... (*Seeing that the room is empty, except for Cuckoo*) Oh, nobody here? Now I'll have to do it all over again ...

Cuckoo never takes her eyes off him. Jerome comes back in from the veranda

(*To Jerome*) Good-morning, I wish to apologize for last night——
Jerome No harm done, Uncle Powell! How d'you feel?
Cuckoo (*quickly*) How d'you feel?

Powell looks at her, then back at Jerome

Powell Amazingly well considering, perhaps it was some sort of catharsis. It's as if there's been an explosion in my head. Now the smoke's cleared away, it feels refreshingly empty.
Jerome Ready for refurnishing?
Powell Exactly. (*Conscious of Cuckoo's steady stare*) What about feeding the swans?
Cuckoo Would you l-like me to?
Powell (*puzzled by her attention*) Very much.

Cuckoo lumbers towards the kitchen, as ...

Lydia comes out of it

Cuckoo Cuckoo feed the swans!
Lydia Good ...

As Cuckoo goes into the kitchen ...

I was too late, she was miles up the path——
Powell Liddy, I wish to apologize for——
Jerome He's better!
Lydia Are you, Uncle Powell? I *am* glad ...
Powell And to go with it ... (*wheeling himself towards the veranda, and*

drawing a deep breath) ... a crisp renewing morning. I've been awake since six. Finding things out.

Lydia What sort of things?

Powell (*going to speak, then hesitating*) You don't want to hear ...

Jerome Of course we do——

Lydia What have you found out?

Powell Two things. First, I've faced the fact that for sixteen years, with your mother's help, I have been playing a part. The hermit, self-sufficient, the cripple-philosopher, in an ivory tower by the name of Kozy Kot. Shedding a patronizing glow over the suburbs. I'm not a philosopher, or even a hermit—I've been as dependent on Mam as Cuckoo was. Her busy hands made my life, and now that life is too empty to be borne. The void has got to be filled.

Lydia (*sitting on the stool*) Yes?

Jerome But your book—you've got that to finish——

Powell That's the other thing. This morning I had a look at "my book". A long impartial look. I tore it up. (*He dips into the drawer in his lap, lifts up two handfuls of the torn-up foolscap sheets with which it is filled, and lets the pieces fall back*)

Jerome But you've been writing it——

Lydia For years——

Powell It's no good. That you know, Lydia, from the passages I've read to you. Turgid, pretentious. No good.

Cuckoo returns from the kitchen, holding a large plate of bread, in small pieces

Powell sinks his head, and looks thoughtfully at the drawer. On her way to the veranda, Cuckoo stops, turns and looks at him in sorrowful pity

Lydia Those swans are getting hungry.

Powell Feed them with this! (*He holds up the drawer*)

Cuckoo P-paper, they'll like that!

Powell (*taking the plate from her*) Give 'em the lot.

As she takes the drawer ...

And if Hickidoola complain you're throwing refuse in the river, that's my look-out.

Cuckoo runs out into the garden

Lydia takes the plate to the dining-table, then sits again

Lydia (*calling*) Don't throw the drawer in as well!

Jerome Uncle Powell ... (*kneeling in the armchair*) ... are you thinking of ... plans?

Powell Based on the fact that I'm not a writer, but a teacher. Before your time, before the war, I was English master at a boarding-school——

Lydia I know——

Powell I was one of the fulfilled ones, give me a blackboard and thirty blank faces and I was happy. Then I was called up. After the war, it was my duty to start fighting—(*designating his body*)—this.

Jerome But be fair—how could you have managed the travelling——

Powell Pupils could have come here, to me! Not in bulk, just six or seven. Once, a parent wrote me that his son had been ill and could I help him to catch up on his English and History in the evenings. I informed him— (*with mounting anger*)—that I was an invalid and too busy writing—*too busy*!—and I sat back into myself and stayed there. That's why, for years, I've hated looking at that school opposite, hearing the children—will you help me?

Jerome Of course——

Lydia I'll go and see the vicar in Hampton——

Powell But wait a minute—how *can* you help, you're going to be married——

Lydia That's all off.

Powell Off?

Lydia We're all as we were.

Jerome It's Cuckoo, you see.

Lydia She'd only be happy here.

Powell Never mind that—who else can we get on to, for you?

Jerome I could have a word with the headmaster over the way——

Lydia Of course. Anything to get you started——

Jerome I'll nip over now!

Powell Now?

Jerome In the dinghy—and I'll tell the headmaster you'll be writing to him.

Lydia Jerome, do——

Jerome Uncle Powell, you're in the saddle!

He runs on to the veranda, almost colliding with Cuckoo as she returns, carrying the empty drawer. Jerome disappears

Cuckoo All gone.

Powell Good.

Lydia (*looking around*) Now what ... Clean sheets—(*to Cuckoo*)—stay in here darling, while I do the beds ...

She goes into the corridor, to R

Powell takes a sheet of paper and a pencil from a slot at the side of his wheelchair

Powell (*calling*) Liddy, what's the next place after this, on the way to London?

Lydia (*off, calling*) Winchford ...

Powell Winchford Grammar, I can write them ...

Lydia returns from the corridor, carrying bed-linen

Lydia Then there's the boarding-school at Painton ...

Powell I'll make a list ...

Lydia goes into the bedroom, closing the door

Benjy comes in from the kitchen, and goes up to get his carpet-sweeper

Benjy, pass me something to rest this on, will you?

Benjy takes up a blotter from the desk, but Cuckoo anticipates him by handing Powell her red book, still open, upside down. Powell makes to rest his paper on it, then looks at the book. He takes it up and looks at the spine

Whose is this?

Cuckoo Cuckoo's.

Powell Oh yes—(*to Benjy*)—one of her father's.

Benjy She's been reading to me. (*He places the blotter on Powell's knee*)

Powell Reading to you?

Benjy (*going*) A fairy tale.

Powell Funny book to read a fairy tale out of. (*Reading, from the cover*) *Examination and Analysis of the Human Stomach.*

Benjy But ... (*showing the place on the page*) ... this bit about the princess an' the dragons ...

Powell (*reading*) "This blocking of the canal can frequently lead to flatulence".

Benjy Thank you.

He looks at Cuckoo, who is sitting looking at Powell

He takes up the carpet-sweeper and goes to the corridor and to Powell's room

Powell writes, then senses that Cuckoo's eyes are on him

Powell (*brusquely, as usual with her*) Yes?

Cuckoo Nothing.

Powell Oh ... Here's your book. (*Turning from her, then back*) You look as if you want to ask me something.

Cuckoo Cuckoo k-keeping an eye on you.

Powell Oh? (*Uncomfortable, turning from her again, then back*) You've never kept an eye on me before.

Cuckoo Cuckoo d-didn't like Uncle Powell. (*Her eyes fill with tears*)

Powell Cheer up—what's the matter?

Cuckoo (*recovering*) Don't let me k-keep you, I'll curl up with a jolly good read ...

She settles back in the armchair and opens the book, as she did with Benjy. Powell turns his chair, to go, then looks at her again, steadily. She turns a page

Powell What does it say?

She looks at him, anxiously, then down again at the book

"What are you nevertheless doing my pretty maid observed our hero ..." (*After a pause, her improvisation faltering*) "I am reading sir she said, and he s-said ba goom she ain't as daft as we thought ... I am reading ..."

Powell You're not, are you?

Cuckoo Not w-what?

Powell Reading.

Cuckoo (*not looking up, stiffening, uncertain*) I am reading ... sir she said ... from my book ...

Powell Yes?

Cuckoo It isn't true. (*Looking up at him, her face crumpled*) Lady Pillie could read to the last d-ditch but Cuckoo ... (*Shutting the book, hopelessly*) Cuckoo *can't read*. Not a word, not a word, not a word ...

Her head falls on the arm of his wheelchair. He puts out his hand, slowly, clumsily, as if to touch her head, then takes it back. She looks up puzzled. He sits, staring; it is as if he had never seen her before

Powell Cuckoo.
Cuckoo What's the matter?
Powell I'm looking at you.
Cuckoo Never happened before.
Powell No, I never have.
Cuckoo What's the matter?
Powell (*after a pause*) I want you to listen to me. Carefully?
Cuckoo Not going to frighten Cuckoo, as per usual?
Powell Have I ... frightened you?
Cuckoo Year in, year out.
Powell You and I have lived in the same house for sixteen years, and have never known each other.
Cuckoo Never been introduced. A lot of years to count.
Powell Between us, we can make up for those years.

Benjy returns from Powell's room holding the carpet-sweeper, on his way to the kitchen

Cuckoo M-make up?
Powell You and I can get to know each other.

Benjy stops and turns to them; he cannot believe his ears

Cuckoo (*after thought*) Once upon a time, Uncle Powell said to Mam, "Cuckoo gets on my b-bloody nerves".
Powell Could be. It can still happen. We'll have to work at it.
Cuckoo Can Cuckoo be your n-nurse?
Powell Of course you can, you're going to look after me! (*Suddenly taking Benjy in, and struck with an idea*) Benjy!
Benjy (*confused, going*) Sorry sir——
Powell Benjy, we have a vacancy!
Benjy Vacancy?
Powell Are you available for a job? As Master of the Household?
Benjy Well sir, apart from a nibble from Buck House, I'm free!
Powell Signed and sealed ... (*To Cuckoo*) Benjy can show you all sorts of things to do in the kitchen——
Cuckoo I can make a cup of tea!
Benjy An' I can show you 'ow to boil an egg, it's easy!
Powell He'll help you to look after me and the house—won't you Benjy?
Benjy Bodyguard, charwoman, putter-to-bedder, keep the table in a roar, I think yew ...

He bows to Cuckoo; she laughs and claps her hands

Cuckoo (*to him, radiant*) Cuckoo going to look after ... (*faltering*) ... after—Uncle Powell.
Powell No.
Cuckoo N-no?
Powell Say "*I* am going to look after Uncle Powell".
Cuckoo (*after a pause, repeating, carefully*) *I* am going to look after Uncle Powell.
Powell And do you know what *I* am going to do for *you*?
Cuckoo What?
Powell Did you ever start?
Cuckoo S-start?
Powell Learning to read.
Cuckoo Mam tried once, then she said Cuckoo got no sin ... sinsintration, did you know?

Jerome hurries in from the garden

Jerome Headmaster not too co-operative, overcrowded, but why couldn't the gentleman have thought of it before ...
Powell Fair enough!
Jerome But I did scrounge this out of him—(*swinging round a small shabby blackboard which he is carrying*)—and a couple of chalks! (*Taking them from a pocket*)

Madam hurries in from her room

Madam Now where is my typewriter, I shall need it in my flat, for the *preparazioni* for my lecture tour—(*seeing the typewriter near the armchair and taking it up*)—ah, *voilà*! (*Turning, and seeing the blackboard*) Good heavens, what is a blackboard doing in here?
Jerome It's from the school across the river ...
Cuckoo From the *school*? The place where they show you how to read?
Benjy That's right—an' this is 'ow—off a blackboard!
Cuckoo Off *that*? (*To Powell*) Show.
Benjy No ducks, not just now——
Cuckoo Show!
Powell Right, no time like the present ... Jerome!

Jerome looks quickly round, decides on the sofa, takes the blackboard and places it at the top end of the sofa, held upright by a cushion. Powell wheels up to it

Madam What is all this? (*Putting down the typewriter, and sitting in the armchair*) *Mamma mia* ...
Jerome Just a second ... (*Going to the bedroom door and opening it*) You're wanted!
Lydia (*off*) What is it?
Jerome Wait and see ... (*He goes to the blackboard*)

Lydia hurries in, carrying a crumpled bedsheet

Lydia (*bewildered*) What's happening?

Cuckoo Show!

She sits on the floor, facing upstage; Benjy puts aside his carpet-sweeper and sits, abruptly, next to her. They are like two children. Powell takes a chalk from Jerome

Powell (*innocently*) Yes, Benjy?
Benjy I jus' want see your spellin's OK sir.
Powell Thank you ... (*To them both*) Now watch. The first letter to get to know. (*Tracing it smartly on the blackboard*) "A". (*Looking at Cuckoo*) Right?

Suddenly, with his handkerchief, he rubs the letter out. He turns to Cuckoo, and holds out the chalk. Cuckoo sways to her feet, looks from him to the others, then at the blackboard

Cuckoo Cuckoo frightened.
Powell No. (*Carefully*) "I ... am ... not ... frightened."
Cuckoo (*after a pause, with an effort*) I ... am ... not ... frightened.
Powell Right.

Reassured, Cuckoo takes the chalk from Powell, and stands beside the blackboard. She looks again from one to the other, then at the chalk. In the silence, she laboriously traces, on the blackboard, a straggling "A". She turns to Powell, eager, anxious, chalk in hand

Powell That was good. (*Rubbing out the "A" with his handkerchief*) Now do it again. (*To the others, particularly Lydia*) It's going to be a long trail awinding ... but it's a start.

Cuckoo turns again to the blackboard, clumsily, lifts her arm and is about to form a second "A" as the Lights fade and——

the CURTAIN *falls*

FURNITURE AND PROPERTY LIST

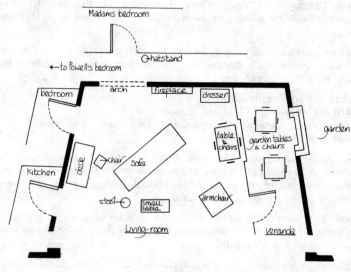

ACT I

SCENE 1

On stage: *Living-room:*

Fireplace. *In grate:* fan of paper. *On mantelpiece:* bowl with box of matches

Dresser. *On it:* china. *Near it:* plant, dinner-gong, tray on end

Table. *On it:* remains of breakfast

4 chairs

Hatstand. *On it:* hats, coats

Desk. *On it:* period telephone, blotter, writing materials, dictionary, books, notepad, pen, envelope, wireless, knitting

Desk-chair

Bookshelves above desk. *On them:* books

Stool or pouffe. *On it:* large doll

Armchair

Small (low) table

Sofa. *On it:* magazine

Oil lamps, ornaments, paintings around room

Veranda:
 Garden tables. *On one:* typewriter, papers, **Madam**'s handbag containing
   powder compact, nail buffer
 Garden chairs
 Bedroom, kitchen and veranda doors open

Off stage: Parcel **(Jerome)**
 Tray with crockery, tumblers, etc. for lunch **(Benjy)**
 Tablecloth **(Madam)**
 Sun-bonnet, handbag containing money box **(Cuckoo)**
 Straw hat, paper streamers, doll wrapped in quilt, abacus **(Cuckoo)**
 Doll, knotted hair-ribbon **(Cuckoo)**
 2 books **(Lydia)**
 Tray with opened bottle of champagne, 5 tumblers **(Benjy)**

Personal: **Benjy:** duster in belt
 Powell: spectacles on cord round neck, wheelchair with rug and tray
   holding books and notebooks (required throughout)

SCENE 2

Strike: Tray with crockery etc. and tablecloth from table
 Tray with champagne, tumblers
 Plant
 Madam's handbag
 Books etc. from tray on **Powell**'s wheelchair

Set: Doll dressed in black on stool
 Different plant by dresser
 Travel labels, pen on table
 Paper on desk
 Large tea-chest half-full of stuff to be thrown away on small table
 2 piles of family albums, letters, photographs, etc.
 1 unsorted pile
 Benjy's jacket on hatstand
 Bedroom, kitchen doors open

Off stage: Pile of old newspapers, waste-paper basket and other debris **(Benjy)**
 Jug with broken handle, torn lampshade **(Lydia)**
 Plate piled with pieces of bread **(Cuckoo)**
 Battered suitcase, lid open **(Benjy)**
 Overnight bag **(Madam)**
 Loaded suitcase **(Benjy)**
 Tray with cups, saucers, teapot, etc. **(Benjy)**
 Empty plate and doll **(Cuckoo)**
 Tea-stand with bread and butter, cakes, etc. **(Benjy)**
 Raincoat **(Mrs Dix)**
 Jug of hot water **(Benjy)**
 Quilt, pill-box hat **(Cuckoo)**

Personal: **Mrs Dix:** handbag with notepad, pencil, half-crown coin

ACT II

Scene 1

Strike:	Tray with tea things
	All cups, saucers, plates, etc.
	Tea-stand
	Quilt
Check:	**Mrs Dix**'s raincoat, **Benjy**'s cap on hatstand
Set:	Stationery, envelopes, pen, **Mrs Dix**'s handbag by typewriter
	Doll dressed in light-coloured dress on stool
	Desk-chair below desk, against wall
	Open book of prints on desk
	Tray with bottles of brandy and whisky (nearly empty), glasses near dresser
	Pack of cards on low table for **Jerome**
	Kitchen door closed

Scene 2

Strike:	Tray with bottles and glasses
Set:	Stocking with needle and thread on low table
	List of numbers by telephone
	Bedroom door closed
Off stage:	Watering-can with water **(Benjy)**
	Apron **(Lydia)**
	Empty coffee cup **(Madam)**
	Tray with teapot, cups, saucers, etc. **(Lydia)**
	Jug of milk **(Jerome)**
	Carpet-sweeper **(Benjy)**
	Drenched hat **(Jerome)**
	Desk drawer full of torn-up paper on lap, paper and pencil in slot at side of wheelchair **(Powell)**
	Plate of small pieces of bread **(Cuckoo)**
	Empty drawer **(Cuckoo)**
	Bed-linen **(Lydia)**
	Carpet-sweeper **(Benjy)**
	Small blackboard, chalks **(Jerome)**
	Crumpled sheet **(Lydia)**
Personal:	**Benjy:** coins in pocket
	Cuckoo: handbag
	Mrs Dix: handbag as before
	Powell: handkerchief

LIGHTING PLOT

Practical fittings required: oil lamps

Interior/exterior—a bungalow living-room and veranda. The same scene throughout

ACT I, SCENE 1   Morning
To open: Bright, general lighting

Cue 1   **Lydia:** "... after tomorrow morning."   (Page 18)
            Fade lights to spot on **Cuckoo***'s back, hold for a second, then fade*
                to black-out

ACT I, SCENE 2   Afternoon

To open: Mellow sunlight

No cues

ACT II, SCENE 1   Night

To open: Interior lighting: oil lamps lit

Cue 2   **Lydia** turns off a lamp   (Page 43)
            Snap off lamp and covering spot

Cue 3   **Cuckoo**, pressed to **Lydia**, sobs quietly, but uncontrollably   (Page 45)
            Fade lights

ACT II, SCENE 2   Morning

To open: Bright, sunny lighting

Cue 4   As **Cuckoo** is about to form a second "A" at the blackboard   (Page 61)
            Fade lights

EFFECTS PLOT

ACT I

Cue 17	**Madam:** "... now you can *see* it!" *Jazz music from punt approaches*	(Page 22)
Cue 18	**Madam:** "That's bad, *cara*, isn't it?" *Music becomes louder*	(Page 22)
Cue 19	**Powell** propels himself to his room *Fade music*	(Page 22)

ACT II

Cue 20	Before CURTAIN rises on SCENE 1 *Light music—continue more faintly, on the river, as action begins, then fade after a few minutes*	(Page 34)
Cue 21	**Jerome** returns from the veranda, frustrated *Noise of chair being overturned, off* R	(Page 37)
Cue 22	**Madam:** "... of course it'll work——" *Loud crash off* R, *then smashing of glass*	(Page 43)
Cue 23	**Benjy** (*in a sergeant-major bawl*): "QUI-ET!" *Feverish jazz music from river, growing louder*	(Page 44)
Cue 24	As Lights fade *Music swells*	(Page 45)
Cue 25	When ready for SCENE 2 *Music melts imperceptibly into sad tune coming from wireless*	(Page 45)
Cue 26	**Cuckoo** switches off wireless *Cut music*	(Page 45)
Cue 27	**Lydia:** "... and look her in the face?" *Waltz music from river—fade after a short while*	(Page 48)
Cue 28	**Madam:** "... can't be done!" *Telephone rings*	(Page 49)

MADE AND PRINTED IN GREAT BRITAIN BY
LATIMER TREND & COMPANY LTD PLYMOUTH

MADE IN ENGLAND